Brend

Chicken Soup for the Soul®

Daily Inspirations for Women

Jack Canfield
Mark Victor Hansen
Marcia Higgins White

Health Communications, Inc.
Deerfield Beach, Florida

www.bcibooks.com
www.chickensoup.com

Library of Congress Cataloging-in-Publication Data
is available from the Library of Congress

ISBN 0-7573-0319-6

Publisher: Health Communications, Inc.
3201 S.W. 15th Street
Deerfield Beach, FL 33442-8190

Cover and inside design by Andrea Perrine Brower
Inside formatting by Dawn Von Strolley Grove

January 1

"I know it's the last minute," Carl said timidly, "but I need a date for my company bowling party tonight."

Two years ago when Carl first joined our church singles group, I wanted to know this man.

Every week my heart fluttered at his warm "hello." We danced together and laughed like teenagers. We stood close together on my deck, watching the city lights flicker, then, abruptly, he said, "I've really got to go now."

"I must be imagining things that just aren't there," I told my best friend.

Carl was a popular guy in our group. In the next year he had his share of dates, but none with me. But then came the telephone call and that "D" word. My emotional alarm clock started to go off, but I decided to give Carl one more chance.

Eleven months later, we were married. During our wedding vows, Carl said, "Thank you for waiting for me." When it was my turn, I shared something I'd tucked away in my heart. It was from one of those dating seminars: "Love is a friendship that has caught fire."

Jan Coleman

Be patient. Timing is everything in life.

January 2

Finding a new job when I moved to another state proved to be more daunting than I'd anticipated. The nurse recruiter suggested I try the new continuing-care facility. Calling a nursing home by another name didn't erase my dismal image about such places, but I felt I owed the recruiter the courtesy of at least touring the place.

On the third floor, wheelchairs lined the hallways as the residents waited to go to the dining room for their noon meal. Dejected faces stared into space. My tour guide cheerfully greeted each resident. As we passed by one old woman, she reached out and grabbed my skirt, holding me in a grip that was amazingly strong.

Suddenly, the cluster of residents became just this one. "What is your name?" I asked.

"Rosemary," was the reply.

As our hands connected, so did my heart. No longer were they pitiful old people, but elderly human beings worthy of my respect and understanding. Tomorrow I will be on duty at my new job. I'll do my best to give compassionate care to each one—starting with Rosemary.

Barbara A. Brady

*W*hen I first met Larry, he came complete with a daughter, McKenna, and a son, Lorin—on weekends. I was completely captivated by my new and charming "instant family," but the children's mother was a different story. I really liked Dia, but our positions seemed to dictate a certain grumpiness with each other that I did my best to squelch.

I watched the children grow, changing from toddlers to schoolkids. And their mother and I continued our civilized and awkward interactions, arranging for the children to come and go, and negotiating vacations and holiday schedules. As the years went by, I noticed that our phone calls changed. I actually enjoyed talking to Dia about the kids. We began a slow but perceptible metamorphosis that was completed the year Dia sent me a Mother's Day card, thanking me for "co-mothering" her children. And while it hasn't always been perfect, I know it's been extraordinary.

One year as we all sat around the Christmas tree, I looked around as the children delivered the gifts. There we were, Dia and her husband, Larry and me, the kids . . . and, surprisingly, I felt at home.

Carol Kline

January 4

grew up with my two sisters on our grandparents' farm in Alabama. Our secret place was near a large pond where we would build our glorious, if temporary, playhouse out of red, long-dead needles of the pines surrounding the pond. Our roofless pine-needle houses usually wound up being about five feet tall; we never felt the need to cover the sky. After we finished building them, we would lie on the ground, facing the sky, and dream. Within these walls, we planned our futures completely, down to the schools we would attend, the homes and families we would have, the places we would go, and the important things we would accomplish.

Through the building of our pine-straw playhouses, we learned that we, like the trees, were sturdier if we grew close to those we loved, and our lives grew taller without the confines of a ceiling. And we learned that everything is more worthwhile and more fun when we share the job, where laughter is shared along with the work. Sharing our dreams helps make them possible.

T. Jensen Lacey

January 5

I met a friend of a friend when they included me in their lunch plans. In the presence of ice water with the freshest twist of lemon and a lunch of hummus on pita bread, this most unusual of creatures turned to me and said, "Tell me about you." I suppose I stammered something about being a nurse or a grandmother or winters in Minnesota.

If I could return to that luncheon table, I would try to talk about the things I wish for and the things that make me unexpectedly happy, or the darkest thoughts I've ever had to sweep from my mind. On those days when uncertainty reigns supreme, I can take myself back and begin, "Let me tell you about me. I'm the one who needs to attend to the conversation that follows."

Beadrin Youngdahl

January 6

*A*nna entered my life behind her son, my new fifth-grader, William. After a brief acquaintance period, I asked if she'd like to help in the classroom.

"I only got to the eighth grade," she whispered.

"Okay," I said, "I'll help you."

Helping her with paper grading began the first of many lessons with Anna. After a while every kid knew that when Anna came, they'd better mind their p's and q's, or suffer the low re-do grade. Then in February of that year, I got a call.

"Mrs. Bucher, I want to help William with his colonial project, but I went to the library with him, and I don't know how to get things done." Of course, she mastered the library system quickly.

The last I heard, Anna was finishing her high-school education, with plans of becoming a fifth-grade teacher. Knowing Anna, she'll do it, and the world will have one more wonderful educator—who grades math with a vengeance.

Isabel Bearman Bucher

The journey, not the arrival, matters.

                                                    T. S. Eliot

_____

_____

_____

_____

_____

_____

_____

_____

_____

_____

_____

_____

_____

_____

_____

_____

_____

January 8

The day started out rotten. She overslept and was late for work. Everything that happened at the office contributed to her nervous frenzy. By the time she got on the bus—which was late and jammed—her stomach was one big knot.

Then she heard a voice from up front boom, "Beautiful day, isn't it?" She could not see the man, but she heard him continue to comment on the spring scenery, calling attention to each approaching landmark. Soon all the passengers were gazing out the windows, and she found herself smiling for the first time that day.

They reached her stop. Maneuvering toward the door, she got a look at their "guide": an older gentleman with a beard, wearing dark glasses and carrying a thin, white cane. He was blind.

Retold by Barbara Johnson

My grandfather had come to America from Greece at the turn of the twentieth century seeking to make a better life. With money in the bank, the time came for Stavros to settle down. He told relatives he was looking for an educated woman from a good Greek family.

Stavroula sat in the chair in the parlor wearing her Sunday finest. "Here," her father said, handing her a newspaper. "Read this when he comes through the door."

"But Papa, you know I can't read!" Stavroula cried.

After the introductions with her parents, Stavros approached the parlor. Completely mesmerized, Stavros knew he would have to look no further. Stavroula would be his bride. She was beautiful and educated.

He bowed to greet her, taking her small, soft hand in his. He never noticed that the newspaper she held was upside-down.

Christine E. Belleris

When you meet the person you will love, you are not blinded by superficialities.

January 10

I helped develop a course to increase the chances of student success in college by building a sense of community within the class. It worked, to varying degrees, until the class from hell that felt it was a waste of time. So I instructed everyone to answer this question on an index card: "If there were one thing in your life you could change, what would it be?"

I collected the cards, shuffled them and handed them out. I then randomly selected students to read the card they held.

One student read: "I wish that my husband's back was better so he could return to work. We have no money."

"I wish my mother didn't have breast cancer," read another. And so on. And so on.

There were tears streaming down the faces of nearly everyone in the class. Without my having to say so, they realized they had far more in common than they had thought. Each of them had problems in their lives. They could relate.

From that point on, the class changed. They worked together. They formed study groups for other classes. They also had another reason to go to college—their friends were there.

Donald Arney

*The real voyage of discovery consists
not in seeing new landscapes,
but in having new eyes.*

Marcel Proust

_____

_____

_____

_____

_____

_____

_____

_____

_____

_____

_____

_____

_____

_____

January 12

One hectic morning, while getting ready for school, both my girls began begging for a new hairstyle. I braided Laura's wispy locks into a snazzy side-braid. I combed Catherine's shiny black hair into a sleek, French twist.

Laura bounced out the door, swinging her braid proudly. But at school, one girl walked up to Laura and asked in a scathing tone, "What's with the stinking braid?" Laura crumbled.

Later, hearing her younger sister's sorrow, Catherine sat in stony silence. I barely noticed that Catherine spent more time on the phone than usual that evening.

The next afternoon I discovered a small miracle had occurred. There stood Laura, surrounded by the smartest, cutest, most popular fifth-grade girls. And, to my amazement, every single one wore a side-braid, exactly like the one Laura had worn the day before.

"I don't know what happened!" Laura explained in the van. "I looked up, and all the girls were wearing my braid."

I glanced at Catherine in the rearview mirror, and I think she winked at me. I'm not sure.

Carolyn Magner Mason

*W*hy doesn't someone tell you what motherhood is really like?

Actually, I had managed rather well with my two girls, but then I thought, *Wouldn't a little boy be fun?* So I was delighted to learn a baby was on the way—until the kindly doctor announced I had twin sons.

As the twins got older, I aged incredibly. Some weeks were worse than others. One day Jeremy learned to open the car door while I was driving. A few days later he leaped from the mantel and needed five stitches in his head. Jon cried for days because he didn't have any stitches and finally consoled himself by drinking iodine. Friends almost stopped coming by, and going out was reduced to a jaunt to the garbage cans or a dash to the mailbox or the clothesline.

Sometimes I wonder how many miles I must have strolled Jon and Jeremy while Julie and Jennifer followed, asking questions. Many times I had no idea how I would do it one more day. Many of my friends and even strangers sometimes quizzed me, "How do you manage?" "I pray a lot," I told them. "I can't make it on my own."

Marion Bond West

January 14

*W*hen my sister was four, she climbed to the top of a Dumpster. Her earsplitting screams made me move at a superhuman pace. I grabbed her, hijacked a skateboard from one of the other kids, positioned my sister on it and set out as fast as my little legs could travel for the next three blocks. I was six.

And it went both ways. At my ninth birthday party, I was flying down a hill when my roller skate caught on a pebble and I was launched. Tawna stepped right in and organized my trek to safety.

Of course, there was the hair pulling and name calling, but when I lost my first love she held me tight and told me I would be okay. When friends treated her badly, I let her vent and told her it would all work out. We carry each other's secrets and hold each other's deepest hopes.

We had to be sisters. We chose to be friends.

Tasha Boucher

*B*ecause getting married was looking like it wasn't in the stars for me, and I wanted to love and be loved, I decided I needed a dog.

I named my puppy Miso. Anywhere I went, Miso came along. If an activity precluded taking a dog along, I wasn't much interested in it.

Looking back, it's remarkable that I met my husband-to-be at all. At first Bob accepted Miso as part of the "package." But as Miso needed to be indoors more due to cold and wet weather, trouble brewed. A crisis point was reached one particularly cold January night when Bob insisted that Miso bunk out on the enclosed porch for the night.

"Don't make me choose between you and Miso," I surprised myself by saying, "because you may be in for an unpleasant surprise!"

Bob wisely backed off. That was a turning point. Bob realized that I did not solely depend on him for love and affection. And Miso found her new place in my life, no longer my one-and-only, but as a beloved member of a family.

Holly Manon Moore

*Someone who loves you will be able
to embrace whoever was important
to you before you met.*

January 16

My daughter Amy was pregnant at seventeen. She decided to place the baby for adoption and asked me to help her choose the parents. The prospective mom assured me, "We want you to be a part of her life." But what role could I possibly have?

The first year I saw Nikki often, fussing over her like any grandparent does. Then the family moved to Florida. As promised, I received pictures and videos of special moments, but how would she ever get to know me from three thousand miles away?

Then the family came to California for a visit. We were to meet at the park. What a delightful, loving child. It was easy to see Nikki was secure, adored by her father and thrilled with two little brothers.

As her other grandmother said good-bye to me, she glanced over at Nikki. "Thank you," she said.

In a minute I understood. Nikki was a gift to Grace that came directly through me. Sitting back to watch me connect with Nikki was Grace's way of honoring me. I put my arm around her.

"Thank you for having room in your heart to let me be 'Gramma Jan.'"

Jan Coleman

*A*t age eighteen I left my home in New York and went off to study in England. It was an exciting but stressful time, especially since I was still learning to cope with my father's recent death.

While at the market one day, I rushed over to help an elderly gentleman having difficulty holding onto his walking stick and his bag of apples. So began my friendship with Mr. Burns. I visited with him twice a week, always on the same days. Although Mr. Burns talked, he allowed me the lion's share.

One day I paid my visit on an "off day." Coming up to the house, I saw him working in his garden, bending with ease and getting up with equal facility.

"When were you able to . . . walk normally again?" I asked, puzzled.

"I guess that'd be the very next day after our first meeting. I saw how unhappy you were, and I knew you needed someone to talk to. I didn't think you'd come if you knew I was fit."

And so the man I'd set out to help helped me. He'd made a gift of his time, bestowing attention and kindness on a young girl who needed both.

Marlena Thompson

January 18

As I prepared to euthanize the black Labrador retriever, dying of distemper, the dog, with great and deliberate effort, slowly lifted her head so that she could look into my eyes. She was not ready to die.

I placed a small bowl of milk under the dog's nose, but she showed no interest in it. I tried again later, and this time she lifted her head and slowly drank. Every few hours I fed her, and the dog's strength gradually returned. When no neurological damage had manifested, I knew my patient was out of danger.

I named her Silky and decided to adopt her. I took her home and was surprised to see her climb onto the bed. When I went to pull her off, she growled and tried to attack me.

Clearly she had been mistreated, and she wanted to know whether I would bully her. Communicating the way I believe animals do—through thoughts and emotions— I held to loving thoughts and images in my mind.

I took her collar and, without hesitation, she jumped down from the bed. Silky has now grown quite old. I'm glad that, years ago, I had the wisdom to pass her test.

Christine Townsend

*M*y wife's sister and her husband became our houseguests during the months between the sale of their first home and completion of the new one under construction. My life became a sit-com with the sheer chaos that goes with having eight people and an insolent house cat living under one roof.

My house is now a combination day-care center/ amusement park. The kitchen has been transformed into a twenty-four-hour diner. Just like in a real sitcom, my wife and I usually end the day giggling about the hijinks that occur during a "normal" day. Like naked babies chasing the cat through the kitchen. Or a naked cat chasing babies through the kitchen. I've never had a sister, but I can honestly now say that my wife's sister is mine.

Chadd A. Wheat

Life can be complicated, but often the complications make the experience more enjoyable.

January 20

During summers when I was young, I would join my grandfather for his evening walk, and he'd tell me how life was when he was a boy.

"Grandpa, what was the hardest thing you ever had to do in your life?" I asked.

"When your mom and your uncles were little, Grandma had to go to a sanitarium. The hardest thing I ever had to do was put my babies in an orphanage. I went every week to see them, but the nuns would only let me watch them from behind a one-way mirror. I'll never forgive myself for not making the nuns let me hold them."

Years later when my grandfather suffered from memory lapses and depression, I tried to encourage my mother to let him come live with us.

"Why? He never cared what happened to us!"

"Mom, Grandpa loves you and always has. He came every week to the orphanage and brought treats, but the nuns wouldn't let him in the room with you."

Not long after, my grandfather came to live with us. At last their love transcended the cold pane of glass that had remained between them for all those painful years.

Laura Reilly

*W*hen she was little, she clung to me and said, "You're my best friend in the whole wide world." She used to cry when I went away for a night or a weekend. "Someday you'll go away and leave me," I would tell her, "and you won't miss me at all."

She's only fourteen now, and though she doesn't know it, mentally she's prepared to go. She came home from school with a homework assignment: choose six people with whom you would choose to be stuck on a deserted island. That night, when she recited the names of the people she would take, there was no mention of me. She chose her brother, her godfather, TV character Doogie Howser, Anne of Green Gables. I never thought for a minute that I wouldn't make the list. I immediately began to sulk.

"You know, Mom, you're being very immature," she told me.

I know I am. But that's because our roles have suddenly reversed. The little girl who clung to me clings no more. Instead I am the one watching her move on and asking, "Why can't you take me?"

Beverly Beckham

January 22

Ever since my five-year-old daughter had fallen off her bike and broken her arm, she'd been afraid. I knew how much she wanted to learn to ride and how she often felt left out when her friends pedaled by our house.

"You know, Hon," I said, "most everything you do comes with risks." I held onto the back of her bike until she found the courage to say, "Let go."

As we walked home, she asked me about a conversation she'd overheard.

"Why were you and Grandma arguing?"

Since my painful divorce, my mother was one of the many people who tried to fix me up. This time she just knew Steve was the man for me.

"Grandma said she just wanted you to find someone to love," she shrugged.

"What Grandma wants is for some guy to break my heart again," I snapped.

"So I guess love isn't like a broken arm," she said.

After I scolded my mother for discussing this with my daughter, I did what I'd seen her do that afternoon: I let go.

Steve was the man for me. We married a year later. It turned out Mother—and my daughter—were right.

Christie Craig

Letting go of what hurt us in the past will open us up to new adventures in the future.

*W*hen my twin granddaughters moved into our house at eight months, my close friend offered me her secret to entertaining grandchildren with few mishaps.

"Teach them the 'one-finger rule.'" The success of the method surprised me.

When my son visited with his fifteen-month-old daughter, I picked her up and said, "Hannah, you may touch anything in this room you want, but you can only use one finger."

I demonstrated the technique, and Hannah followed my example. If she started to grab, I gently reminded her to use one finger.

Months later, my husband and I visited their home, and I watched Mark and Kim continue to practice the one-finger rule.

The night before we returned home, Mark sat on the floor stuffing gift packets for his potential clients. Hannah helped.

Then she picked up one gift, stretched her prize to me and said, "One finger, Nana!"

Linda Osmundson

January 24

My very first teaching job was leading a vibrant group of four-year-olds. At the end of my first day, I was called to the director's office. A parent wanted to enroll her daughter who was born with a birth defect that required she wear leg braces from the knees down.

That night my stomach was in knots. How could I take on a child with special needs?

The next day Kelly's mother carried her daughter into my classroom and set her down on the edge of the carpet. After several days of carrying her to and from the yard, I asked Kelly if she would like to try walking down the hallway by herself.

The next day Kelly began her first journey and made it ten feet. Each day Kelly continued her slow walk down the corridor. I charted her progress with pencil marks on the wall. After several weeks she made it all the way to the yard.

When her mother brought her to school after her annual checkup, she asked if I'd been forcing Kelly to walk. Then she gently lifted Kelly's dress to show me that her knee braces had been replaced with ankle braces.

Seema Renee Gersten

Love is shown by deeds, not by words.
Philippine Proverb

_____
_____
_____
_____
_____
_____
_____
_____
_____
_____
_____
_____
_____
_____
_____
_____

January 26

On the night of her fifty-ninth birthday, Helen Weathers suffered a brain aneurysm. Her family waited through a six-hour operation to see if she would survive. When she started recovering, Helen was almost like a child. Although everyone wanted her back, it became clear that Helen might never be the same woman again.

She was placed in intensive therapy, and after seven months, she made it home to her husband and dogs.

"I am convinced that the only reason I was spared is to inspire others," Helen says. She receives dozens of calls a day from people seeking help with similar disabilities, and she never turns anyone away. She knows deep in her heart that love and caring guided her out of the storm and helped her wade safely back to shore.

Helen Weathers as told to Diana L. Chapman

People can survive against all odds with the love and caring of family and friends.

*W*hile delivering laundry into the appropriate bedrooms, I stumbled upon my 13-year-old sister's diary. I had always been jealous of my little sister. I competed with her tacitly and grew to resent her natural abilities. I felt it necessary to shatter her shadow with achievements of my own. As a result, we seldom spoke.

I tentatively plucked the book from the floor, convinced that I would discover scheming and slander. It was worse than I suspected. I was her hero. She admired me for my personality, my achievements and, ironically, my integrity. She wanted to be like me. I ceased reading, struck with the crime I had committed. I had expended so much energy into pushing her away that I had missed out on her.

I longed to know her again. I was finally able to put aside the petty insecurity that kept me from her. On that fateful afternoon, I decided to go to her—this time to experience instead of judge, to embrace instead of fight. After all, she was my sister.

Elisha M. Webster

January 28

My friend Rita celebrated her fifty-fifth birthday on January 28, 1998. Forty-five years earlier she was scheduled to be on the local *T-Bar V* television show, but months before the big event, social workers came to her home and removed her and her brothers from an environment deemed unacceptable for children. The years went by and Rita grew up, married and had her own child, who also grew up.

At age 54 she finally told a friend about the painful parts of her history. The friend suggested she write Randy Atcher of the *T-Bar V* show and tell him how much it would mean to get a birthday card from him.

The mail came on her birthday, but no card. Rita was at her son's house for a birthday dinner when the doorbell rang. Randy Atcher walked through the door.

Rita shed tears of joy as her daughter-in-law brought out a huge cake while Randy sang the *T-Bar V* birthday song:

"Happy, happy Birthday from all of us to you.

"Now you'll have happy birthdays all your life through."

And Rita knew the words of the song were true. At last.

Marie Bunce

It is never too late to live out one's dream.

*M*y sister found Jake roaming the streets, all skin and bones, filthy and exhausted. Although the vet didn't expect him to live more than a week, Jake was still with me after a month. That was when I noticed a newspaper article requesting dogs and volunteers for a pet-assisted therapy program. Jake passed the tests with flying colors and became an official hospital volunteer.

One particular visit stands out. A man asked if Jake and Mac, his partner, could visit his wife who was very ill. I took her clenched fist and let her knuckles stroke Jake's ear, and when I looked at Jake, I knew he'd made a connection.

Upon hearing that this patient was awake, the nurse told me I must have the wrong room. The woman who was talking and hugging Mac had only 5 percent of her brain function and was not expected to wake up.

My dog, and others like him, had a power that left me in awe. It's simple: My dog Jake worked miracles with his love.

Terry Perret Martin

January 30

I would be facing motherhood as a single woman, so I wanted to start with a new and innocent baby who could ease me into the trials and joys of parenting. Then a girl's image on the television demanded my attention. "I need a mom who can help me become a young woman," the 12-year-old said. And I surrendered myself to adoption.

The call I finally got was for a boy whose mother was a drug addict. Michael was in the hospital with a broken leg. "We think his foster mother did it," the social worker told me.

Ultimately, it was Michael's younger brother and sister that I was able to adopt. My daughter was born addicted to heroin. Both she and her brother have seen more grief than someone three times their age, and they require medication just to behave normally.

My kids are demanding. They will get right in your face, screaming in frustration, then turn around and cling to you, arms squeezing the breath out of you. "I need you," they're saying. "Can you love me?" And I answer with satisfaction, "Yes, I love you."

Pamela J. Chandler

*S*etting: a school in rural Arkansas where the first-grade students would participate in a different kind of reading program. After they had successfully completed a book, they were allowed to take books and tapes home over the weekend. They were to return the items on Monday.

On Monday, Nicole didn't bring back the book and tapes. For three weeks she either said she forgot or didn't offer any excuse at all. Then one day, Nicole's young mother came to talk with the teacher.

Her first words came haltingly. "When Nicole told me she was learning to read, I didn't believe her. Nobody in my family can read. When I asked her how she did that, she told me she listened to the tape and followed in the book with what the teacher read.

"The reason Nicole didn't bring her reading stuff back was because I just couldn't let go. I had to find out if I could learn."

For Nicole's teacher this was confirmation of what she had been taught about teaching: So many wondrous things seem to come about by accident. And this mother, who believed that she was too dumb to learn, actually read to her mother.

James Elwood Conner as told to Carla Merolla

No one is ever too old to learn.

February 1

The bitterest tears shed over graves are for words left unsaid and deeds left undone.

Harriet Beecher Stowe

_____

_____

_____

_____

_____

_____

_____

_____

_____

_____

_____

_____

_____

_____

_____

_____

I had worried myself sick over Sergei's mother coming to see me. I was a new teacher who gave honest accounts of the students' work. Sergei was extremely bright, but his grades were awfully low. I felt I was being called to account for his poor work.

I was completely unprepared, therefore, for her kisses on both my cheeks and her thanks for helping Sergei become a different person.

I wondered how I had made such a life-changing difference to that boy. And then I remembered the day when I encouraged another student to project her voice. "Speak up," I said. "Sergei's the expert on this, and he can't hear you in the back of the room." I realized that the boy who most needed praise was the one who took the last seat that day.

I became kinder that day and much more careful of what I say in front of students. I understood how fragile our children are and how a small kindness can indeed make a life-determining difference. I hope Sergei did well in life because he gave me more than I gave him.

Molly Bernard

February 3

watched a tapestry in the making in a hospital room the other night. The first threads were woven together 53 years before when Mac and Asa Lee dated, fell in love and were married. They reared a son and a daughter and enjoyed the arrivals of five grandchildren over the years. Then Mac's health began to fail.

I met Asa Lee when several of us from our church stopped at the Veterans Administration Medical Center to sing carols.

Mac suffers from congestive heart failure and Parkinson's and also has an eye condition that has robbed him of most of his sight. He didn't seem to recognize his wife.

Our singing done, we started for the door. I saw Mac turn his head with great difficulty and reach toward his wife. She instantly returned to his side and grasped his outstretched hand, bending near to give him another kiss.

The clasped hands and shared kiss spoke of a love that had knit together the joys and overcome the pains of a 53-year tapestry of love and devotion as ancient as creation and as new as tomorrow's sunrise.

Vicki Marsh Kabat

*D*ay 1: I'm starting a diary about the kids' upcoming experience with chicken pox. Vicki called to tell me her kids have chicken pox, and when I looked at the calendar and counted the days, it turns out my kids will have chicken pox right in the middle of our school's break. Plus, my husband is already planning to stay home that week to catch up on paperwork, so why not just get it over with?

Day 2: Went to grocery store to stock up on calamine lotion.

Day 18: School break is over; daughters back in school. Husband back at work. Son home with chicken pox.

Day 21: Daughter erupting with chicken pox.

Day 26: Husband left for out-of-town business trip. Son now has flu. Second daughter also home with stomachache.

Day 30: All kids home from school—one with chicken pox, two with flu, one faking to get in on the snacks.

Day 32: Husband called early from nice hotel. Very understanding when I was unable to remember his name.

Day . . . So tired. Don't know what day it is and don't care anyway.

Janet Konttinen

February 5

As a savvy seven-year-old, I knew that in life you got what you didn't want. We had recently lost our dad, and now, after 13 years of staying at home, Mom had to go out and look for a job. Not only had she little education, but she had limited experience and no special training.

She was unable to hold on to the home that Dad had built, and the family car disappeared into the night. Mother's options were further limited to jobs that were within walking distance.

As Christmas approached, Mother asked us to talk to Santa, which was the only activity you could do for nothing at the school festival. I decided to tell the truth. "I wish my mother would get a job so we can buy groceries."

A few days after the holiday, my mother received a phone call. "I've been offered a job in the school lunchroom."

I found out that Santa Claus, whether he is your grandpa in a red suit or the school superintendent doing his bit, is not such a scam after all. From then on, I told younger kids that if they didn't believe, they were really missing out.

Jean Bronaugh

Sometimes wishing can make it so.

*W*e were sitting in the crowded auditorium waiting to view our seven-year-old grandson's performance in his school's annual pageant. Then I saw them—Tanner's "biological" paternal grandparents.

Even though my daughter-in-law never married Tanner's father, his parents had fought for grandparents' rights and won. His court-ordered visits with them every other weekend had always been a particular sore spot for me.

The program started, and before we knew it, the lights were on, and we were gathering our things to leave. When it was our turn to hug Tanner and discuss his job well done, he said, "Grandma, I'm so lucky because all my favorite people are here, together, just to see me!"

My eyes met those of the "other" grandma and I could see she was feeling the same shame as I was. What had given only me the right to love this little boy? They obviously loved him as much as we did, and he obviously loved each of us. I discovered that night that we all have the same agenda—to love a little boy who truly belongs to all of us.

Patricia Pinney

February 7

When my husband died, I had never done anything on my own. Instead of sitting home and crying over my loss, I decided to go to college. It was the scariest decision I've ever made, but the exhilaration of learning new things was worth it.

The age difference between the other students and me wasn't a problem, and I received a great deal of attention from many of my teachers. My daughters were very supportive and even helped me with my homework.

I learned I could study abroad and met some wonderful people who took me under their wings. I had mastered another step in being on my own.

Looking back, I realize that going to school kept me young. I was never bored. I was exposed to new ideas and viewpoints. Most important, I gained confidence, realizing I can accomplish things by myself.

And so it was, that with a flick of a tassel, my lifelong dream was fulfilled. At the age of 68, I graduated from college—with honors.

Mildred Cohn

Don't let fear hold you back.

February 8

*M*y twin boys were only seven when their paternal grandmother announced she was remarrying. We broke the news to our boys.

Jon looked thoughtful for a while, then finally asked, "Is she going to have more children?"

Before we had a chance to respond, his twin brother Mike shot back this answer: "No! She can't. She already had them. It's like chicken pox. Once you get them, you can't get them again."

Susan Amerikaner

February 9

*J*ustin was my sister Roxanne's first child; two years later, Shaun was born. When Roxanne divorced, I moved in to help so she could work and go to school. Later I moved out, and Roxanne met a man I didn't care for (an IV drug user) before finding Tony, who loved her and the boys. But something was happening to Roxanne.

"It's advanced AIDS," the doctor said.

"Rhonda, I want you to take my boys," she said to me.

I wasn't there when Roxanne told the boys that they were losing their mother and would be leaving their home. Two weeks later I was awarded custody.

As Roxanne worsened, I knew I had to be strong for the boys. At church I met Jerry; Roxanne must have thought, *This man may raise my children.* The boys stood at my side as Jerry and I took our vows.

Today, if we're out and someone says to the boys, "Your parents . . . ," I always correct them. "We're Aunt Rhonda and Jerry," I say. I could never take Roxanne's place—and I don't want to. I just want to raise the boys to be the fine young men she wanted them to be.

Rhonda Adkins as told to Carla Merolla

**Sometimes we must help carry out
other people's dreams
when they can't do it themselves.**

*O*ne lazy afternoon while watching my children play, I started thinking about how differently the world looks through the eyes of an adult with so many responsibilities. Suddenly I felt a pang of longing for the days when I, too, could romp and play without a care for cost-of-living increases, budgets and mortgages.

I let my children reteach me that afternoon how much fun it is to squish fresh mud into patties, and how thrilling it is to climb just one branch higher in a tree and then from your perch in the sky, gaze over your tiny kingdom and yell, "I'm the king of the world!"

It took only a few stolen moments from my children's youth to remind me how precious these carefree days are for them. Now, instead of reprimanding them over and over about this and that and giving lectures on appropriate behavior, I enjoy the moment with them. You see, I've been taught a lesson the children haven't learned yet: The moment won't last forever.

Stacey Granger

*W*hen Delores, a dainty little cat, came to live with her owner, Kyle, she rarely had anything to say. Most of the time, she didn't even like being touched. She also became upset whenever the lights were turned out, so Kyle just left the lights on in the apartment at night.

Then, one evening, everything changed. Kyle woke up to something jumping on his head! Paws were scratching his face! When he opened his eyes, his apartment was filled with black smoke.

Kyle felt for Delores with his feet and followed her to the back door. The knob came off in his hand. Kyle collapsed to the floor. Once again, he felt those insistent paws scratching on his face. He hurled himself against the door, broke it down and ran outside to fresh air and safety. But Delores was still inside.

An hour later the blaze was under control. A firefighter brought Delores—eyes seared shut, hair singed—wrapped in a towel.

The fire changed Delores. She meowed and purred constantly and wanted to be touched and cuddled. Kyle had never asked for more than Delores could give and then found she was willing to give him everything she had.

Susan McCullough

*S*ome of the lowest days of my life came shortly after my husband's death. The kids and I each grieved as our ages and personalities allowed. And then, my sister arrived. She had saved her visit until everyone else had left. Within hours, the closeness we had shared in the past came flooding back.

We got my kids returned to school and then started tackling projects. We decided to install a closet organizer since the half-emptiness constantly reminded me of my now-gone husband.

Things didn't go well. Nothing fit. As we improvised, things got worse. Then somehow the whole situation turned into a joke.

Every fumble we made, every board that slipped, every screw that refused to twist made us laugh. We laughed until the tears came. It was the first time I'd laughed in weeks.

That laughter changed nothing, yet it changed everything. For in the hard months following my sister's departure, on my worst days, I inevitably opened my closet and spotted my slightly tilting organizer. No matter how I felt, I just couldn't help smiling.

Deborah Hedstrom-Page

Laughter can help heal the pain of loss.

February 13

The kindergarten teachers told me Benjamin wasn't like other children; he didn't like stories, he couldn't sit still, and he didn't have respect for other people's property. It became my mission to help him relate to other children, feel safe and secure in school, and learn to read and write.

In time, most kids began to accept Benjamin, but no one besides me called him "friend." He learned some social skills, but he wasn't able to concentrate on learning. I sent him to second grade feeling like I failed him.

At the whole-school assembly on the first day of his third-grade year, Benjamin told me, "I'm goin' to listen 'cause I wanna learn." And incredibly, he did learn to read that year.

Because of Benjamin, I don't think I'll worry about students in the same way. Although I hadn't taught him to read as I had hoped, somehow I had helped prepare him for learning. And I knew that Benjamin knew that.

Dori Courtney

February 14

*I*n 1944, among 8 million people in New York, Nathan and Evelyn fatefully crossed paths. They met when the soldier from Texas was on leave visiting the Big Apple. Nathan used each of his five passes to see Evelyn. Before he shipped out, they had vowed to write daily, and over the next 16 months, they sent each other 1,100 letters.

Everywhere his unit was sent, Nathan carried with him in his one duffel bag the hundreds of letters Evelyn had sent. When he returned home, they were married in Nathan's family's synagogue.

Fifty years later they renewed their vows in the same synagogue. "World War II brought us together," Evelyn said. "In Hebrew, we have a word, *beshert*—divinely appointed, meant to be. That is what Nathan and I are, *beshert*—we are each other's perfect soul mate."

And the 23-pound package of letters Nathan had sent home from the war, along with the letters Evelyn had lovingly saved, were compiled in book form as a labor of love to pass along as a special legacy for their children, grandchildren and friends.

Amy Seeger

You have to work at love, especially when circumstances get in the way.

February 15

I'd never noticed how tall he was until I stood between him and the objects of his anger. I knew that he played varsity football, that he carried a weekly progress report, and that slipping marks could disqualify him from play. But he was doing well in my class.

We'd been studying the Civil War, and today we'd been watching excerpts from Ken Burns' Civil War documentary. At one particular moment, the students were riveted to the scene on the television screen: a recalcitrant slave's gruesomely welted back. The room was hushed, except for two obnoxiously giggling boys in the back-row corner desks.

Eric erupted like hot lava, challenging the boys with his fists. I moved quickly between them. "Please . . . ," I soothed, "please sit down." Minutes passed. The bell rang. The two boys, scared silent by his anger, exited the far door. As he and I stood squarely facing each other, I sensed the impotent torment of the young black male who stood before me.

I had known his anger before. But until now, until today, I had not known his anguish.

Willanne Ackerman

I didn't grow up with cats, but I married a cat lover. We first saw Turtle on our land in Vermont, trotting behind her mother. She reappeared briefly a year later, and the year afterward, she visited often. As Turtle grew more comfortable with us, I wondered if we could bring her inside.

The deciding moment arrived after I'd been away for a few days. Barely fifteen minutes after my return, she was at the kitchen door! When my husband opened the door to bring her some food, she pushed past him into the kitchen and headed straight for me. She had missed me! I was ready to share my house with her.

Turtle had a lot to learn. How to sprawl across my in-basket. How to awaken us for her breakfast. How to stand guard at the bathtub until I could be meowed safely from the water. I bless the day that she decided to chance it with us. She knew so much more than I did about the important things. She knew enough to make a running leap that day into my house, my lap, my heart.

Ellen Perry Berkeley

Open your heart to love,
no matter where it comes from.

February 17

As I watched my sister unload my luggage, I could see the sadness in her eyes. We had both been dreading this moment for the past week. One last hug and a final good-bye and I would be on my way to a new life abroad, leaving her behind.

On the plane I was still crying. I did not have the energy to put my bag in the overhead locker, so I stuffed it in the empty seat next to mine. The plane shook heavily, and the bag fell on the floor. I bent over to gather up my belongings when I saw an unfamiliar little book. It was a diary. The key had been carefully placed in the lock, so I opened it.

I recognized my sister's handwriting. She had been keeping a diary for the past month, and she was now passing it on to me. I was to write in it for a couple of months, then send it back to her.

Even though an ocean separates us, it felt like she was actually there. It was only when I thought I had lost my best friend that I realized she was going to be around forever.

Martine Klaassen

February 18

He has not learned the lesson of life
who does not every day surmount fear.

Ralph Waldo Emerson

_____

_____

_____

_____

_____

_____

_____

_____

_____

_____

_____

_____

_____

_____

_____

_____

February 19

Clara Barton was on the battlefields of Cuba for the Spanish-American War and founded the American Red Cross at the age of 51. She did not let age get in her way, going wherever there was suffering to relieve—after battle, fire, flood, earthquake or yellow fever. A woman of commitment, she continued to fulfill her mission through her golden years until she died at age 91.

One day, someone reminded her about an offense that another person had committed against her years before, but she acted as if she had never heard of the cruel act.

"Don't you remember it?" her friend asked.

"No," came Clara's reply. "I clearly remember forgetting it."

Amy Seeger

Let go of the cruel things people do to you.
Put them out of your mind.

February 20

*W*ith 20 years of marriage ended, I was now a single parent convinced there was nothing beyond this dismal, dark moment in my life.

My daily two-mile jog temporarily lifted my spirits, so I didn't want to miss it, even though a radio bulletin warned of rapidly approaching thunderstorms, hail and high winds.

As I emerged from the leafy tunnel that marked my usual turnaround point, I saw massive black clouds boiling up. Although every step was agony, I kept going until only one long, steep hill lay between me and the safety of home. Suddenly, a terrible roar filled my ears, the ground shook, and I was knocked flat on the ground. I gasped for breath as lightning struck a tall metal fence post at the edge of a field and a ball of fire rolled across the ditch, blinding me with its glare. Trees bent double in the wind. I lifted myself on all fours, ready to take my chances against the elements, and made it to my car. I was alive!

Nothing would ever be the same again. Confronting death made me realize the preciousness of life; I intended to live it to the fullest.

Maggie Baxter

February 21

*You cannot make yourself feel something
you do not feel, but you can make yourself
do right in spite of your feelings.*

Pearl S. Buck

_____

_____

_____

_____

_____

_____

_____

_____

_____

_____

_____

_____

_____

*W*e were at Disney World, and our two children were clamoring for sunglasses. Rob, who was five, picked out Donald Duck glasses, and Lauren, three and already into fashion, chose pink Minnie Mouse glasses. They wore them up Main Street and into Fantasyland. They took them off and clutched them in their hands when they went on the rides.

Somehow, somewhere, the Donald Duck glasses disappeared, and Robbie cried. "If you had loved them, you would have taken better care of them," we said to him. Lauren offered, "You can have mine, Robbie." But he didn't want hers. They were pink and for girls.

A few months ago we were in Orlando visiting our son—long an adult. In the flurry of rental cars and restaurants, he lost his sunglasses. We didn't scold him. Instead, we did what most adults do for other adults: We helped him figure out where he could have lost them.

I know that as parents we have an obligation to teach our children. But I also know that everything doesn't have to be a lesson. Sometimes, lost sunglasses are just what they are: lost sunglasses and nothing more.

Beverly Beckham

Don't look at every mishap as a life lesson. Sometimes accidents are just accidents.

February 23

As Mercy Hospital's three-to-eleven nursing supervisor for 40 years, I experienced just about every medical emergency.

Late one evening, I was paged by the emergency department saying a mom was about to deliver her fourth child while en route to the hospital. I hustled to the ER driveway just as their car pulled in.

I opened the door to the passenger's side to find the young mom leaning back in the seat, groaning and pushing—with three little boys gawking over her shoulder from the back seat. With one more groan and push, the infant was in my hands.

As the staff rushed up with medical supplies, I heard one little boy gasp, "Now I know where babies come from!"

His little brother responded, "Yeah! From under the car seat!"

Elaine Stallman

February 24

My eyes filled with tears as I kissed my son, daughter-in-law and precious grandchildren good-bye at the Sydney, Australia, airport, knowing I wouldn't see them for at least two more years.

But on this visit Tracy and Phillip had talked incessantly about their new computer and how, if I bought one, we would be able to communicate daily.

And so it was that I abandoned my outdated typewriter and made a frightening leap into this fast-paced, high-tech era of e-mail.

The machine became my nemesis and the hero that could link me to my family. By e-mail, Phillip tells Gramps and me about his role in the school play and his test scores in math. And we were in on Tracy's tenth birthday plans from day one.

The kids write when they're happy, and when they are hurting. They share some secrets they don't even tell Mom and Dad, and they ask me questions that only a grandma could answer.

I still make lots of mistakes on my computer, but then Tracy says, "I love you guise bigger than the entire world!" For that I'll take any abuse this whiz-bang wonder of chips and a motherboard dishes out.

Kay Conner Pliszka

February 25

*W*e had five children, and their activities kept both Steve's and my hands constantly busy. Then Steve died, and I lived with the stress of being both father and mother and trying to provide for all their needs.

One evening my children and I were gathered around the dinner table. I began to talk about hands, how my hands were so busy. I reached out my two hands and asked each child to take hold. There were so many of them and only one of me that we sat transfixed, realizing there was no way I could meet all their needs.

A small voice broke the silence. "Mommy, if we all reach out to each other, we could each get a whole hand."

We began to smile.

I'm still a single parent of five active, intelligent children who have had to grow just a little bit stronger. They don't reach out solely to Mom for help; they reach for each other, as well. With those ten extra hands, our family is now a circle of help and support. We have enough hands to go around.

Linda Butler

*O*n my fiftieth birthday, my older daughter gave me a pin that said, "Fifty is nifty." I wore it to work that day, and what fun it was! All day long people kept telling me I couldn't be 50. Didn't look 50.

It was wonderful. I knew they were lying, and they knew I knew, but isn't that what friends and coworkers are for? By the end of the day, I felt fabulous.

Arriving home, I had just shut the front door when the doorbell rang. It was a young girl from a florist shop, bringing birthday flowers from a friend. As the delivery girl waited for her tip, she noticed the pin on my jacket. "Oh, fifty, eh?"

"Yes," I answered. I could stand one last compliment before my birthday ended.

"That's great! Birthday or anniversary?"

Anita Cheek Milner

February 27

I was no fan of bedtime. When Dad came home I'd lie there and listen to my parents fight.

Soon it was Kathleen's voice I heard. "Don't be afraid. Come and get in bed with me."

Decades later when I was on the verge of my own divorce, my sister invited me to live with her. "You need a comfort zone right now."

We were both teachers, and every day after school we walked six miles. I vented; she listened.

At the end of the school year, she followed her heart to the ocean. Mine led me to the mountains. Yesterday I had a touch of the blues. My family and friends seemed so far away. As I was trying to get over myself, the phone rang.

"Hi, Sweetie!" I felt the arm around my shoulder as surely as if she were standing in the room with me. We talked for an hour. When I hung up, I was wrapped in her familiar comfort zone.

Melinda Stiles

Sometimes we can overcome our own fears when someone else needs us to be strong.

rincess Misha, our Siberian husky, had an innate love of the outdoors, and, of course, the cooler the better. On warm summer evenings, she would stretch out on the cool cement of the front patio. One night we watched her suddenly stand up, walk over to a toad that had hopped out of the grass, pick it up in her mouth, then walk back to her resting place and lie back down. She put her chin on the walk, opened her mouth and let the toad out. The two stared at each other for some time, then the toad hopped off into the grass.

We watched this same phenomenon repeated over the next two summers. One night we watched as a large toad hopped out of the grass. Misha gently laid down her head so that her nose almost touched the toad. Could it have been the same toad all along?

Misha had surgery that summer, and we kept her indoors to recuperate. One evening, there was Toad (as we called him) on the porch, staring through the screen door.

We laughed about the incongruous friendship, but maybe in her stalwart toad, Princess Misha had found her Prince Charming.

Joan Sutula

March 1

I once taught in a small, private school. One morning the headmistress made an announcement to all the children gathered. "Today we begin a great experiment of the mind." She held up two small ivy plants, each potted in an identical container. "We will give them the same amount of light, the same amount of water, but not the same amount of attention," she said. "We will put one plant in the kitchen and one on the mantel in this room. Each day we will use our good minds to think good thoughts about this plant on the mantel, and we won't send any to the plant in the kitchen. And then we'll see what happens."

Four weeks later my eyes were as wide and disbelieving as the children's. The kitchen plant was leggy and sick looking, but the Great Room plant had increased threefold in size with dark, succulent leaves.

The kitchen ivy joined the other ivy on the mantel, and within three weeks, the second plant had caught up with the first.

I took this lesson to heart: All things grow ... with love.

Joan Bramsch

Love and attention make all things grow.

March 2

Seven months out of my marriage, I had met the "great love of my life." We dated a year, and with my divorce final, we planned a trip to Europe. Two weeks before takeoff, he took off, leaving me with two small children and facing my ultimate fear: life alone.

I decided if I was going to be lonely for the next few years, I might as well be lonely in Europe.

I arrived at the train station in Paris, the highlight of my journey, panicked and disoriented. I had arrived in the most romantic city in the world alone, lonely and petrified. I knew that if I didn't go out, right then, and find a place to have dinner, my dream would be foregone, and I might never learn to enjoy the world as a single individual.

I wore out two pairs of shoes during my week's stay. I returned home a believer in the healing power of solitary travel. Traveling alone redeems itself by demanding self-reliance and building the kind of confidence that serves the single life well. Now when I meet an obstacle, I just say: If I can go to Paris, I can go anywhere.

Dawn McKenna

March 3

*I*t was a summer's evening when my husband Tim left me a young widow with a daughter to raise. As I struggled to work through the grief and pain, I surveyed the large garden that Tim had put so much of himself into. I couldn't possibly keep it up, so I decided to make an herb garden out of it. It was something that I could lose myself in.

In the strawberry bed I planted a white birch. It became the Tim Tree. In the spring, with the help of a friend, I put down wood chips; another friend brought plants I'd never seen or heard of.

Although the garden was taking shape, I still felt lost and toyed with the idea of selling the house and moving. That is until the afternoon I stumbled right smack into my epiphany.

The garden had made me remember what I had tried so hard to forget: I loved this place where Tim and I had started our journey, and while that part was over, the journey has continued.

The pain has gone from my memories now, leaving them full of laughter and warmth. The healing garden has lived up to its name.

T. J. Banks

One is not born, but rather becomes a woman.
Simone de Beauvoir

_____
_____
_____
_____
_____
_____
_____
_____
_____
_____
_____
_____
_____
_____
_____
_____
_____
_____

March 5

Unk played the "fiddle," but never when anyone was around. Except Eleanor. They'd been friends 70 years. Neither married.

Eleanor sang in choir, served at suppers, sewed for the Ladies' Aid. It was rumored she played harmonica, but not in public.

Unk was 79 when Eleanor died. The church was full for the funeral, but Unk didn't come along when we left the house. Reverend Winters read scripture. Roberta Gerrity spoke for the choir. A man spoke about what an inspired Sunday school teacher she had been. A long silence followed.

That's when Unk limped down the aisle, fiddle in his left hand, bow in his right. He began with "Amazing Grace," slipped seamlessly into "Greensleeves," then wove strains from both into a sound more mournful and sweeter than any I've ever heard. The whole church cried as Unk walked out and trudged home.

He played in his room every night after that, until his dying day. And many a night, I swear I don't know how, Unk made that fiddle wail and cry, just like a harmonica.

Steven Burt

*Love and devotion do not end
with someone's passing.*

Dear Grandchild,

*G*randma and Grandpa know that you're hurting right now because Mommy and Daddy are breaking up. This time is difficult for us, too.

We want you to know several important things that we hope will help you to go through this scary and difficult time.

The first thing is: It is not your fault.

Second: You probably can't fix it.

Third, and maybe most importantly: We will never divorce you! We will always be there for you when you need us.

You might think that you'll never be happy again, but we want you to know something we've learned because we've lived so long and seen so many things—you will laugh again; it will get better. Good things will happen.

Here's a list of things you can count on:

· Nothing you can ever do or say will make us stop loving you.
· We'll be good listeners for you.
· We'll give great hugs and warm, long back rubs.
· We'll still make your favorite foods.

Honey, you're not alone. Your mommy and daddy still love you, and we'll always love you, no matter what.

Love,
Grandma and Grandpa

Hanoch and Meladee McCarty

March 7

Communicating with our patients can be a real challenge. Do they really understand what we're asking?

One young man, for example, called the hospital, shouting, "You gotta help! My wife is going into labor!"

The nurse said, "Stay calm. Is this her first child?"

"No," he cried urgently. "This is her husband!"

Maybe to communicate more clearly, we simply need to ask for what we need.

A new patient at the clinic finished filling out his health history form. The nurse noticed that under "sex" he checked both "M" and "F"—then wrote in "and if I'm feeling strong enough, sometimes on Wednesday, too."

Maybe patients just can't hear us.

One man boasted, "I have a new hearing aid."

"What kind is it?"

"One o'clock."

Karyn Buxman

*O*ften, after she finished her solitary supper, she would sit at the kitchen table, remembering how everyone used to rush off after they had eaten—the boys up to their rooms and Peter to his favorite TV news programs. But now that the boys had left and Peter was gone, she would have given anything to have those frenzied days back again.

On what would have been her fortieth anniversary, she baked the chocolate blackout cake that had been Peter's favorite, and there it sat, in the refrigerator.

Last year the boys had all called, and they had talked about how would they celebrate the big 4-0. But how could you observe a wedding anniversary with half a couple? Suddenly, Max the dog began barking. She flung the door open, and there were her three boys, standing there.

"I didn't think you'd remember, and besides, with Dad...." Her voice trailed off.

"Ma, you and Dad were always here for us, and every anniversary will be our special day."

Suddenly, she smiled and ran back to the kitchen, thanking the divine force that had directed her to bake her cake today and had given her three wonderful sons.

Evelyn Marder Levin

**Share special memories
with the people you love.**

March 9

My father had died before I was two. My mother had to walk to work every day, bring three loads of coal up 17 steps and light a fire to keep us warm. When I was about 13, I got a job at a local department store on the weekends. I earned 23 cents an hour and was to get paid just before Christmas. I wanted to get my mother something special that year. One evening I saw it. The moss-green satin lounging pajamas and matching robe cost $25.95—a fortune in 1950.

Two nights before Christmas, I watched as the saleswoman wrapped the soft satin gift. My mother said it was the most beautiful thing she'd ever seen. Through the years, even after they'd fallen apart, she would tell people about those pajamas.

Many years later, the demands of raising a family had begun to show on my face and in my attitude. Mother was visiting us one Christmas. We were knee-deep in paper when she handed me a large golden package. Inside was the most elegant pink-and-gold silk lounging robe I'd ever seen. She, too, must have remembered those green satin pajamas and known how desperately I needed that robe.

Marion Bond West

had always wanted to go back to college. I had dropped out in my senior year, and it had been a long time since I had "cracked a book." Shortly after graduation, I attained my teaching credentials. And because I loved to learn, I decided to go for a master of arts degree in education and creative writing.

Graduate school was exhausting and overwhelming at times, but the next two years flew by. I was in my final quarter with only one class left to take when I was diagnosed with cancer. My professor suggested that I do my work in Los Angeles where I had to go for radiation therapy, mail it to him, and we could keep in touch by telephone.

My graduation day was special because I had finished my radiation treatments and my schoolwork.

To this day I continue my journey down the avenue of learning. My students are now my greatest teachers. In my quiet times, I write my thoughts and feelings on a clean sheet of paper. I take each day and live it. Life doesn't get much better than this.

Lola De Julio De Maci

*Take each day and live it.
It's the best way to enjoy life.*

I had nine underclass players excited that they had a chance to play in a baseball conference game scheduled when our seniors would be out of town on a field trip. The most excited was Billy, a mentally challenged boy who had received special permission to be on the football and baseball teams.

Somehow we went to bat in the bottom of the ninth within one run of our opponents. To our surprise, with two outs, a batter walked, and the tying run was on first base. Billy was our next hitter. With a two-strike count, Billy hit a triple to tie the score. The crowd went wild. I called a time-out and whispered instructions to Billy. When the catcher threw the ball back to the pitcher, Billy broke from third and dove headfirst into home plate, beating the throw and scoring the winning run.

This memory exemplified what sports can do for people, and Billy's great day proved that to everyone who saw the game. J. M. Barrie may have said it best when he wrote: "God gave us memories so that we might have roses in December." Billy gave all of us a rose garden.

Herb Appenzeller

Give everyone a chance.
They can surprise you by how well they do.

*O*ne day in second grade, I asked to be excused from class. I walked to the fourth-grade class and asked to talk with my sister. In tears, I whispered, "I forgot my lunch."

Without hesitation, my sister grabbed her brown bag and handed me half of her peanut butter and jelly sandwich, half of her crackers, half of her grapes—even half of her oatmeal cookies!

"Here, take this," she said.

"Are you sure?" I asked.

She smiled and nodded yes.

Years later, I stood up for her in her wedding, and she stood up for me in mine. When she became pregnant, I was preparing for my fourth surgery: a hysterectomy.

This time my loss was bigger than a lunch, and my sister couldn't rescue me. Still, when she and her husband asked my husband and me to become legal guardians of their newborn daughter if something should happen to them, across the years my heart could hear her say, "Here, take this."

"Are you sure?" I asked.

She smiled and nodded yes.

Penny Perrone

*L*ife begins at 70! I thought being 60 was incredible, but being 70 is almost incomprehensible. I can relax. People don't generally expect as much of me.

When I was in my sixties, people expected me to retire to a rocking chair on the front porch of a condo. I didn't feel guilty when failing to meet their expectations. Now, I am considering retirement, but nobody asks me about it anymore.

By the time you are 70, your kids are old enough to recognize that you did the best you could as a parent and no longer hold you responsible for their problems.

Being 70 also gives me more perspective. I've learned not to sweat the small stuff. It's all small stuff. Life is very precious, and it shouldn't be wasted on hate, bitterness or holding grudges. I am convinced that doing good will keep my heart and mind strong and vibrant.

I do not know what the rest of my life will bring, but I am setting goals and planning for it to be a great adventure.

Paul J. Meyer

*Think of life as a great adventure
and never stop setting goals.*

*S*ix months old and barely three pounds, Necco wasted no time establishing herself as the one in charge of our lives. The leather chair was her scratching post. The Christmas tree was her playground. It happened that her skills reached their peak just as my life reached a low point. My marriage ended, leaving me with a 10-year-old daughter and a large home to support. I soon realized I would have to work as a freelance writer just to meet expenses. That meant getting up at 4:00 A.M.

The routine lasted exactly two weeks. Depressed, I began sleeping through the alarm until finally, I quit setting it.

That's when Necco did a curious thing. She decided that the perfect time to make the kind of noises that made a human jump was at 4:00 A.M.

Every day Necco got me up when the ideas were freshest and the world slept around us. Stories were born, polished and sold. Today, my daughter and I are fine, and the old house still surrounds us. Whenever another story is sold, I give thanks to my muse—a little cat with a mischievous grin, who kept me company in my "darkest hours."

Cindy Podurgal Chambers

March 15

The shadows of the evening run deep while love comes in to soothe every mind and body.

Kabir

_____
_____
_____
_____
_____
_____
_____
_____
_____
_____
_____
_____
_____
_____
_____

*G*eorge Blair overcame his family's poverty caused by the Great Depression and survived two potentially paralyzing accidents to water-ski his way into near-legendary status in this country and abroad.

He became the first person to water-ski—barefoot or otherwise—on or off all seven continents. He attributes his seemingly inexhaustible energy to exercise and a sensible diet. One small component to George's diet is the banana—which he considers God's most nearly perfect food.

He still has all kinds of goals. "I can't wait to test myself with the next goal, with the next accomplishment. My problem is that there are not enough seconds in each minute or enough minutes in each hour to do what I want to do."

George's advice to 60-year-olds: "There is hope for all of us. Every day I try to do a little better. And you ought to, too. Start easy, but go for it. And set goals."

Robert Darden

***Setting goals lets you test yourself
so that every day you do a little better.***

March 17

Once my husband and I started living on a ranch, I began to appreciate our Hereford cows on a deeper level. I began to recognize them by their different markings, personalities and habits and even gave them names.

I was puzzled the first few times I saw a single cow surrounded by several calves, until I learned that herds establish unique baby-sitting co-ops. One day I was astounded to see that Red Man, our huge 2,500-pound bull, had been persuaded to baby-sit.

One night, we woke up to the terrifying sound of coyotes on the hunt. That morning we found one dead calf, which we covered until we could bury it. I watched as the mother nudged her baby and stood bawling. Soon 11 other cows formed a circle around them and began to bawl with the mother. The cows stayed in that circle of love for over an hour until finally the mother backed away and walked to a far corner of the pasture.

As I watched them, I, too, became a member of their circle. I stood rapt and motionless, feeling the depth of their compassion in my own heart, and filled with awe and admiration for these animals.

Maria Sears

*O*ur house is very often visited by relatives who come from out of town and spend two or three weeks with us. Recently, we had a relative come to our house late one evening. It was a young lady. She came about three and a half months ago and is still with us. We are very much inconvenienced as her habits are very different from ours.

She likes to sleep during the day, and at night she keeps us awake to amuse her. She has her meals regularly enough, but they are not at the same time as ours, and this is a big problem. She smiles when in good humor with such a broad and pleasant smile we can't help but smile back at her even though she has disrupted our lives completely. In spite of all of these things, we hope that she never leaves for we love our baby sister very much.

Joseph Brandes, 12 years old,
three months after the birth of his baby sister

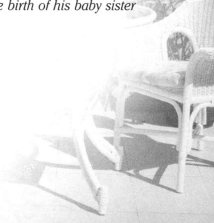

March 19

I watch as Grandpa paces his domain, strolling through the rows of young growing plants, testing and touching and studying.

"Come here, Sweetheart. I have a surprise for you." I hurry after him.

He stops at the last row. I stand back as he lifts the broad leaves aside, searching for his surprise. It is a small, still-growing pumpkin, still attached to the vine, and I can see a scar on the far side.

Then Grandpa turns the pumpkin over, brushing the dirt away, and I can see that it's not a scar at all; it's my name, growing there along with the pumpkin! MY NAME!

"How did you do that?" I asked.

"Well, it's a long process," he begins. His eyes sparkle as he discusses magnifying glasses and special planting techniques.

We begin the long walk back to the house. And I think about my very own pumpkin and my grandpa who can work magic in his special garden. I place my hand in his and walk up the hill to breakfast.

Kati Dougherty-Carthum

Learn to let go.
That is the only key to happiness.

Buddha

_____

_____

_____

_____

_____

_____

_____

_____

_____

_____

_____

_____

_____

_____

_____

_____

March 21

I've never lived alone until now. At 70-plus, I am in complete charge of my home, my cat, my car and myself.

I have learned that lunch can occur anywhere from 11:00 A.M. to 2:30 P.M., and dinner anytime from 4:30 to 10:00 P.M. I can eat fully dressed or in my pajamas and socks.

Bedtime is another adjustment, although I haven't moved to the center of the bed since my cat prefers the right side. But if I awaken in the night, I can read or view a movie without disturbing anyone.

I have to admit there are some negative aspects to living alone, such as eating the same meal two or three times until the leftovers are gone, or having to remove the dead bird from the dryer vent myself.

And, I have, in fact, established a new identity—not daughter, wife, mother or grandmother, but a separate person in my own right—ME—still a work in progress.

Louise Hamm

I heard his footsteps before I saw him; his shuffling feet never left the floor. He looked awfully sleepy and needed a shave—not unusual for 3:00 A.M.

He approached the nurses' desk and asked, "What are they gonna do with the pony?"

"What pony?" I answered.

He began telling me they should put him down at the far end of the meadow and let him eat the yellowed cornstalks left from this year's crop.

I tried to reorient John as to his whereabouts and see the reality of the nursing home. As I gazed into his cloudy blue eyes, I suddenly recognized how much better his reality was than mine. He was in a meadow with a new pony. I was trying to place him within the stark walls of an institution.

I patted John on the shoulder. "I think that the far end of the meadow would be perfect."

He continued shuffling down the hall, smiling.

Mary Jane Holman

March 23

woke up feeling cranky. I didn't want to do housework, read the work I brought home from the office or do anything that resembled responsible behavior. As I drank my tea, I thought I felt a headache coming on. Maybe I was coming down with the flu. I didn't really want to be sick. To be truthful, all I wanted was a little time off. Did I have to wait to be sick to do that?

I talked to myself. *Okay,* I said, *you need a day off. Admit it. Accept it. Toss out the guilt and enjoy a mini-vacation.*

In the bathroom I lit a vanilla-scented candle and stepped into the bathtub into which I'd poured a half bottle of bath gel. With a grateful sigh, I immersed myself in my homemade spa.

By late afternoon, I was back at it, refreshed physically, mentally and emotionally. I had given myself permission to listen and respond to my needs, to care for myself the way I tended to my family. I didn't need illness to justify a rest. It was such a simple awareness, but then isn't it the simple things that set us free?

Ferida Wolff

Take time out to do something enjoyable for yourself.

*I*n my previous life, before I was reincarnated as a mother of three, I wore clothes that fit and matched. I read *Time* magazine and the newspaper. I had a career and friends who were more than three feet tall.

In my previous life, I was free. I could carve my own path and follow my dreams. Now, I endlessly rearrange piles of laundry, crumbs and toys. I am pulled and tugged, hassled and harassed, stepped on and sat upon, and desperate or in need of some solitude. I am bleary-eyed and graying, underpaid and overwhelmed. Sometimes I wonder who I am and what I've become. Then, one of my children shouts, "Mommy, I need you!" and it is perfectly clear.

I am the center of the universe. I am MOM.

Gayle Sorensen Stringer

Becoming a parent can mean losing who you were—but becoming something much more important instead.

March 25

My grandmother Miriam knew the most amazing things. She could spell Mississippi backwards and keep an omelet from sticking to the pan.

We were kindred spirits. I told her we'd travel around the world together, and she showed me how to touch the stars by closing one eye and balancing them on my fingertips.

She was the first person who ever encouraged me to dream and to put those dreams down on paper. Her lessons are the ones that stuck with me: She taught me how much constitutes a pinch of salt, how to use seltzer to get a stain out of a silk blouse, and helped me appreciate the simple things, like the quiet moments at dusk when the whole world is draped in a curtain of blue light.

As I stir a big, boiling pot of stuffed cabbage on my stove, I can picture Miriam sprinkling a dash of sugar for sweetness and squeezing in just enough lemon juice to "give it a kick."

And I can't help thinking that "life is like that"—sometimes sweet, sometimes sour, and always a challenge to blend both parts perfectly.

Sheryl Berk

*A*s I got closer to motherhood, thoughts of my own mother came more and more frequently. She had died of cancer when I was 13. After she died, I missed her with a bottomless ache in my soul that never went away.

I got a second mother in my wonderful mother-in-law, Ethel, but she died three years before I got pregnant. As my baby grew inside me, I felt keenly the fact that I had no mother to help me.

A few months before our baby arrived, my husband and I decided to hang a picture of each of our mothers on the wall so our son could "know" his grandmothers.

For me, labor lasted 33 hours and ended in an emergency C-section. When I woke up from the delivery, I was groggy and in pain, but I couldn't wait to meet Ben. He looked at me for the first time, and I saw my mother's eyes—big, deep brown and full of sparkle. And there's a funny little skin fold under his eyes—just like Ethel.

I have been blessed with a beautiful son whose smile gives me back both of my mothers every day of his life.

Nancy L. Rusk

March 27

My gynecologist was seeing a pregnant patient who had brought her young daughter to the appointment. The young girl had toted along numerous toys, and as the mother hopped up on the exam table, the gynecologist made conversation.

"My, you have a lot of nice toys there," he said.

"I brought them for the baby," she replied.

"Well, how is the baby going to play with them now?"

The girl replied, "I thought while we were here, you could put them in there for me!"

Lynne Murphy

*W*e knew we could not be with Matthew to celebrate his second birthday, so we made a short video. When my daughter reported the success of the video, I began doing them whenever we saw or did something that we would have done with Matthew had he lived closer. It was a good way to keep from being strangers and was also a learning experience as we showed him things that might not be readily available in his area.

The "Grandma Videos" have continued for over seven years now, and four more grandchildren are viewing them. The videos are obviously unprofessional, but the children certainly don't mind. We sometimes wonder if we enjoy them more than they do. It's fun for us to look at things from a child's perspective, and I find we have a renewed interest in the simple little objects we often took for granted.

My own children saw their grandparents only once a year, but ours can literally have their grandparents at their fingertips anytime they wish.

June Cerza Kolf

March 29

My husband brought our three young children through the maternity ward, pausing to let them wave at the new mothers cuddling bundles. At my room, he beckoned them in and introduced them to their new brother.

Five-year-old Katrina fingered the baby's thick red hair, inspected his little feet, admired his tiny ears and planted kisses on his dimpled elbow. But her coos stopped short at his wrist.

Drawing back, she pointed at the identification bracelet and frowned, "Look, Mommy. They left the price tag on!"

Carol McAdoo Rehme

I first met Jeanne on moving day. Recently single again, I was forced to move from my dream home to a small duplex, and my spirits were about as high as the grass in the front yard.

But Jeanne was doing the single lifestyle well, and her zest was contagious. Every year I hung out with her, the more I laughed, and the less I thought about the past and how it hurt and robbed me.

Then it happened. I met Carl. Nobody but Jeanne and I could understand that though our friendship would remain as deep and faithful, sadly it would never be quite the same.

The night before the wedding, I wrote Jeanne a long letter full of memories of all the special things we did together, and how she would always be my best friend.

Life has seasons, and we must change with them as best we can. It's been four years now, and Jeanne hasn't found her Mr. Right, but she's not sitting around waiting. She makes every day count, and she still motivates me to do it, too.

Jan Coleman

***Friends can motivate us
to be the best that we can.***

March 31

*S*ome day, when you're as big as me, you may not remember your preschool teachers. But I want to help you understand how much you mean to me.

You have taught me what it's like to be a kid again. I've learned to sing and dance again. I know how many blocks you can stack before I have to yell, "Look out!" as they come crashing down. I know that "even if your hair is sticking out, scissors are for cutting paper." I've learned that bubblegum toothpaste tastes better than mint, and that markers are better than crayons.

I've also learned what it feels like to be loved like only a child can love, and I've learned that it's one of the best feelings in the world. I've learned how fast you grow and how quickly you change.

But most importantly, I've learned how wonderful children are. And although you will very vaguely remember who I was, please know that I will always remember you.

Jennifer L. DePaull

It happened on an early September morning. As I came out the front door I saw her, out in the middle of the road. Dancing. My neighbor. A mother. A wife. Otherwise, quite mature. Dancing in her pajamas and robe, and wearing her giant furry-dog bedroom slippers. Sipping on coffee, curlers in her hair. Dancing and all alone, to the tune of some music only she could hear.

I stopped dead in my tracks. She saw me staring and laughed, and giggled and danced some more. And then she called out to me: "I have four children, and this morning, my youngest just went off to her first day of school. I'M FREEEEEE!" And she kept on dancing.

Raymond Aaron

April 2

The small ad said, "Literary agent moving to Houston—out of New York—to be where the writers are."

I made an appointment with Mr. Hudson. After telling him about myself, beginning with third grade and including an overview of my current novel, he said, "You're just the kind of author I like to take on. I'm planning to go to New York to hand-deliver a manuscript for another author. Maybe I can come back with two advance checks."

Three weeks passed, and I phoned his office. No word. Six weeks passed and the receptionist was straightforward. "Mr. Hudson said to tell you that your manuscript doesn't quite have the … potential … he's looking for."

I scolded myself for even thinking I had the ability to write a novel—until two months later when I saw an article about Mark Johnson, alias Paul Hudson, alias Jack Zimple, moving from state to state scamming would-be authors.

Many years and 37 published books later, I still recall the value of this experience: Don't ever let somebody else tell you the value of your work.

Dianna Boo

Circumstances can make you doubt yourself. Don't give up.

No pessimist ever discovered the secrets of the stars, sailed to an uncharted land, or opened up a new heaven to the human spirit.

Helen Keller

_____

_____

_____

_____

_____

_____

_____

_____

_____

_____

_____

_____

_____

_____

_____

_____

April 4

On my first trip to Alaska, I met Mike. He had been a full-time student at the University of California in Riverside when he was struck by a car. The accident left him a double amputee. His parents had taken him on the cruise to celebrate his return to school after ten months in hospitals and rehabilitation facilities. When we said good-bye, I promised Mike I would keep in touch, and that I would try my best to get a cruise donated to the trust fund his family had set up to cover the cost of his prosthetic limbs.

In 1998, he took his first steps with his new prosthetic leg. Unfortunately, right before his last quarter of school, Mike developed bone spurs from his new leg. Just weeks before his graduation, he was refitted with another leg and had to learn how to walk all over again. Despite all his obstacles, Mike still managed a 4.0 GPA!

Less than two years after meeting Mike on that Alaskan cruise, I was traveling from Chicago to Riverside, California, for Mike's graduation.

Cindy Bertram

*S*hortly after learning I had a rare type of breast cancer, I decided to cut back on some of my activities. I became upset as I told my son's classroom teacher about my diagnosis and the long months of treatment that lay ahead. "Know what your rope is, Myra," she counseled. "And hold on. Whatever it is. Just keep holding on." It didn't take me long to figure out that my rope would be the love of my family and friends, who I knew would support me through whatever lay ahead.

As my treatment progressed, that rope was there during chemotherapy when my husband said, "Lean on me." It was there one night after I had lost my hair, and I found 50 cents under my pillow with a note from the "hair fairy." On those occasions when I didn't get along with the people whose support I desperately needed, it felt as though the rope was slipping out of my hands.

I survived my journey. I often hear my friend's words echoing in my mind: "Know what your rope is, Myra." I do, and I'm still holding on.

Myra Shostack

Turning to others for support in a difficult situation is what will get you through it.

April 6

My parents came to visit me while I was serving as a Peace Corps volunteer in the Philippines. Approaching my little hut, my parents grew quiet as they took in the seemingly impoverished human condition of my life. I had already been living on the island for over a year and was not prepared for how this lifestyle might appear to a "more comfortable" mind, especially my father's.

At night, we retired to the comforts of my bamboo floor and the darkness. Mom and Dad cringed in horror at the sounds of rats and mice scuttling, lizards chuckling, palm-sized spiders leaping and carnivorous cockroaches gnawing just beyond the flimsy mesh barriers of their mosquito nets.

When dawn arrived, we were up at the crack of it. Water needed to be fetched, food scavenged for, laundry soaked and scrubbed.

The day before my parents departed, we had lunch at a hotel. I glanced over at Dad and asked him what was wrong. He looked deeply at my mother and said, "We've seen so little of the world, other people, other customs, other ways of living. Thank you, Leah, thank you for opening our eyes."

Leah Burgess

"*L*iving with a writer is like living with Dr. Jekyll and Mrs. Hyde," I hear my husband tell our neighbor. "There are more ups and downs than in the astronaut program."

"How come you've stuck around so long?" Bud asks.

"She promised to buy me an airplane—a real one," my husband says. "She tells me about famous authors and their humble beginnings. Did you know Stephen King was rejected a hundred times before he sold a thing? By my count, only forty-four rejections to go and the plane is mine!

"It could be worse," he continues. "I could be married to a psychiatrist and become paranoid overnight. And I doubt she'd promise me a plane."

I smile as I turn back to my work, knowing my husband understands a little about this writing life. He's a modern kind of guy and can take care of himself. He knows where to find the cream of broccoli soup.

It's right next to the cream of chicken.

Judith A. Chance

April 8

"Why are there more pictures of Lisa than there are of me?" our younger daughter asked.

Marilyn said, "I've never counted them. I don't know."

Lori turned and left the room. Caught off-guard by the question, I mumbled, "There can't be that many more pictures of Lisa than of Lori."

"When Lisa was born, you were taking photographs. When Lori was born, you were involved in colored slides," Marilyn replied. "There must be hundreds of slides of Lori somewhere in the house."

Later that afternoon, when we were alone, we went into the basement and found the trays of slides. Over the next few days, we went through them all, selecting and rejecting pictures until we were satisfied. Then we converted them into photographs and placed them in an album.

On Lori's birthday, I left the album and a birthday card in her room, explaining why her mother and I had put it together. Later that morning I answered my office phone. A tiny voice spoke with obvious difficulty. "I love you, Daddy," she said and disconnected.

Alvin Abram

$\mathcal{M}$y husband was diagnosed with congestive heart failure at age 46. One day my closest friend stopped by and knew that I was having a tough time. She hugged me, and I said, "Sometimes widowhood doesn't look bad." And then I never thought of it again and never felt guilty about it.

Several weeks later, my oldest daughter and I had an argument. Her father backed me up. I approached her later. "I will not have you upsetting your father and risking him dying."

Melanie screamed, "I don't care! I wish he was dead!"

The next day he was.

Despite counseling, Melanie's wound closed, opened and festered. For her eighteenth birthday, I decided to give her three things: a bag of party balloons (for the ups and downs in her life), a set of darts (to throw at my picture) and the board game Life. "You will learn that Life is not a game, until you are old enough to discover that it really is." And, describing what I had said to my friend that day, I told her, "You never did anything that I had not already done. I never had anything to forgive you for."

Mary-Ann Joustra Borstad

April 10

Dear John,

I must confess that your son—my new grandson—and I made a pact that very first day you brought him home from the hospital. When no one was looking, I took his warm little fist and freed his fingers so they could wrap around one of mine. I remembered how you, my own brand-new baby, had also held on tightly. I knew that we had made an agreement, sealed with a secret handshake, acknowledging that both of us would let go when the time was right. Then it seems that I merely blinked and you were letting go, long before I thought you would.

I could lament your passing youth and my own. For now, though, I'd rather relish completely the thrill I got as my precious new grandson gripped my finger and stared intently into my eyes. I know he was telling me he'd trust us to hold on, to teach him what he needs to know of life, to be there as long as he needs us. Then we'll all let go with our hands, but continue to hold on tight with our hearts.

Love always,
Mom

Lynn Stearns

Although we have to let go of our children one day, we will always keep them close in our hearts.

April 11

*N*othing could have prepared me for the rugged terrain of Chile's Torres del Paine National Park in Patagonia.

I had arrived in Santiago as planned to meet my 73-year-old husband, Larry, who had been backpacking on his own through the park. But Larry didn't show up.

Park rangers began a search, and a month later, Larry's body was found.

Because I wanted to get a sense of what my husband was feeling before he died, I made arrangements for a seven-day trek with two guides. After ascending cliffs, descending over rocks, and fighting through mud and vines, we arrived at the spot where Larry's body was found.

I created a makeshift marker out of some stones and sat in silence. Soon my tears weren't of sadness but of joy in celebration of the wonderful life we had together. From Larry, I had learned to persevere in difficult circumstances and to accept the challenges with a sense of humor and always with a strong sense of adventure. This journey was a summation of Larry's life spent tirelessly in pursuit of challenges, both intellectually and physically. These seven days and 70 miles were a tribute to his boundless spirit.

Adele Carney

April 12

From quiet houses and first beginnings,
out to the undiscovered ends,
there's nothing worth the wear of winning,
but laughter and the love of friends.

Hilaire Belloc

_____

_____

_____

_____

_____

_____

_____

_____

_____

_____

_____

_____

_____

_____

_____

*W*hen my best friend moved to a town three hours away, I was devastated and, of course, wrote about it in my column.

Susan and I had known each other for five years. She was my first real neighbor, and we'd been close for longer than the lifetimes of our children. We both had stories—long, drawn-out epics—we shared weekly. Every morning our cars passed as we brought our boys to different schools. The sight of her car, of someone else doing what I did, boosted my own self-esteem. It took weeks before I stopped looking for her car.

About the time I was recovering from my loss, a woman hailed me in the grocery store. "My best friend just moved away, and you said what I felt, but I didn't have the words."

I was lucky; someone actually confronted me with the power of my work. It made me realize that in the end, writing is not about the money. It is about giving a single person, one reader, the right words.

Catharine Bramkamp

**When we share our feelings with others,
we can help them give voice to their own.**

April 14

I have flown hundreds of flights since I became a flight attendant for a major airline, but I will always remember one particular flight from Los Angeles to Washington, D.C.

I answered a lavatory call light in the coach cabin and found a young mother struggling with her infant.

She was on her way to deliver the son to the family that was adopting him. She could no longer support the two of them. They had spent the previous night on the airport floor because they had missed their flight and had very little money.

The other flight attendants brought cloth towels to clean up both mom and infant. I gave her a sweater and pair of pants I had brought for my layover. Then I asked several families if they could spare extra diapers, formula and clothes for the child.

Once we landed, I walked them to their next flight and briefed the new flight attendant crew on the situation.

As she thanked me, she said softly, "You're a sky angel."

Whenever I look at my "angel wings," I'm reminded of that day when I learned we are all spiritual beings traveling in human form.

Robin Chapuis

We are all spiritual beings.

My father loved honeybees. Over the years he built up a large apiary, which eventually provided a major portion of our family income. Because a hive of bees could die of starvation during the winter, beekeepers helped their bees survive by feeding them syrup made from sugar and water.

During World War I, our nation rationed sugar, honey was in great demand as a substitute, and beekeepers were given an extra ration to keep their bees alive. When some favorite relatives were coming to visit, we begged Mom to take enough sugar from Dad's bee ration to make one of her beautiful cakes.

A few days later it was time for our family of seven to receive our monthly allotment of sugar. When Dad got home he set the tiny brown bag on our table. Mom took out the amount of sugar she'd used for the cake and poured it in the bee sugar barrel, leaving a scanty amount for us. Mom made no fuss over it. It was just a natural action on her part, in keeping with the integrity with which my father and she lived their lives.

Mildred Bonzo

April 16

Euphoria was ours the day my friend Carol and I received the $2.98 jars of bust cream. After the recommended ten applications, Carol was definitely developing—thanks to the cream or Mother Nature. But the proof was there.

So, one sultry July day, I made the second most important purchase of my teen life: falsies. Carol and I hurried home clutching the bag that held my soon-to-be new figure. Carol assured me I looked like Marilyn Monroe.

We left for the park swimming pool. We dove into the cool water and swam and swam, until I noticed one falsie floating by without a care in the world. Embarrassed beyond belief, I ran into the girls' locker room and changed back into my clothes.

When Carol and I arrived at my house, Mom could tell that my little corner of the world had ended. Through tears and sobs, the shamefaced tale was told. "Go get my sewing basket," Mom said, "and we'll fix things right."

That afternoon Carol and I learned that the quick answers to problems were often false, but love that was shared around the kitchen table was often the truest love of all.

Alice Collins

**Be patient. Quick fixes to problems
usually don't work.**

*M*y father was a municipal bond attorney who nurtured a passion of a different sort—writing. Probably the most important advice he ever gave me was how to handle rejection: "When disappointments come along, as surely they will, don't stiffen with bitterness. Bend with the wind. When the adversity has passed, you can right yourself again."

Not surprisingly, I began a lengthy love affair with the written word. In college I wrote poetry and short stories. At 22, I started work on my first full-length novel. It was never published, nor was my third.

Without knowing it, I was teaching myself three vital lessons about writing: persist, persist, persist. Eventually, I was supporting myself and my children writing numerous movies for television. I also had seven novels that never saw the light of day.

My father had set aside his publishing ambitions and renewed his commitment to municipal bonds, thinking that when he retired he would return to writing. He died at the age of 71, four months before the publication of my book, *'A' Is for Alibi*, teaching me yet another lesson: Summon the courage to live out your dreams. None of us really know how much time we have left.

Sue Grafton

Live out your dreams.

April 18

If we have no peace, it is because we have forgotten that we belong to each other.

Mother Teresa

_____

_____

_____

_____

_____

_____

_____

_____

_____

_____

_____

_____

_____

_____

_____

_____

_____

April 19

The countless flyers announcing those missing after the September 11 attack were everywhere in my downtown New York neighborhood. Written on them were desperate and loving words penned in moments of almost unimaginable anguish by people whose husbands, wives or parents had simply not come home. Like many of my neighbors, I spent much time in silent and sympathetic contemplation of these heart-rending pieces of paper.

The flyers reminded me of Tibetan prayer flags, flapping in the warm breeze. (Also called "wind horses," their purpose is to purify the air with the prayerful words written on them.) It was almost too much to bear. And yet we, the neighbors and friends of these people, felt duty-bound to bear witness, to pay respect, to send love and light.

Marc Farre

April 20

It is Day 118, and I am alone in the middle of the Pacific Ocean, attempting to be the first person to row around the world. I want to lament about sun blisters, unfavorable currents and winds, jellyfish stings, saltwater sores and the ever-present loneliness.

I open my laptop computer and open a message from my wife. It contains an extra message from a couple in Chicago.

> I saw your story on television and find your spirit incredible. My wife is in the hospital having a bone-marrow transplant. We find inspiration in your journey, and we pray for you daily.
>
> Rick and Susan

I am embarrassed. I have a couple of blisters and a few aches and pains, while Susan's lying in darkness and can't move. She's got cancer. I have a jellyfish sting on my foot.

I log out and put my computer back into its watertight case. I fix dinner and eat in silence, surrounded only by the slapping waves of the ocean and the courage of a couple in Chicago. The boat feels lighter. My destination feels closer.

Mick Bird

*Names have been changed.

Learning how others face their challenges can give us the courage to deal with our own.

$\mathcal{M}$y friend Michelle is blind, but you'd never know it. I really realized this the first time my six-year-old went to play there.

When she came home, she was very excited about her day. They had baked cookies and played games, but she was especially excited about her finger-painting project.

"Michelle told me my picture showed joy, pride and a sense of accomplishment. She really saw what I was doing!" Kayla said, and that's when I realized she didn't know that Michelle was blind.

When I told her, she was quiet for a moment. Then Kayla said slowly, "You know, Mommy, Michelle really did 'see' my picture. She just used my eyes."

And I knew that my child was right because Michelle had listened to Kayla describe her artwork, heard Kayla's pride in her work, wonder at her discovery of the way colors blend and her delight in the texture of the medium.

I've never heard anyone refer to Michelle as handicapped. She isn't. Hers is a special type of "vision" that all mothers could use.

Marsha Arons

April 22

Meg, Katie and I sat rocking on the swing on Meg's front porch, caught up in Meg's description of the heart surgery she would undergo in two days. When Meg's dad called her in, I hugged her tightly. "I'll be praying for you," I said.

Meg did not make it through the surgery.

On the way to the funeral home, I kept telling myself that Meg was okay, but when I saw Meg lying there, reality hit. I missed Meg terribly.

One evening several weeks later, Katie and I were walking when we found ourselves heading for Meg's front porch. We sat on the swing, talking quietly, when the front door opened and Meg's mom came out.

"I was hoping you girls would stop by. Please keep using the swing. Meg's dad put it up for the three of you, and we hate to see it empty."

We scooted together, closing the space that had separated us. "Do you suppose there are porch swings in heaven?" Katie asked.

"I'm sure of it," I said. "And I'm sure Meg will be saving us a place on one when we get there."

Teresa Cleary

April 23

When my three boys were just wee ones, my unmarried high-school friend invited me to visit in her new condominium. After lunch we sauntered into her living room to sip our coffee and reminisce. I was immediately struck by the fact that there wasn't any peanut butter oozing down the kitchen cabinets and no Kool-Aid puddle on the kitchen floor. When I approached her bathroom with caution, I found no potty seat on the toilets and there wasn't a turtle or frog to be seen in the tub. Driving home, I felt vaguely sorry for myself.

No one was in the yard when I pulled in. The kitchen was noticeably free of dirty dishes, and the boys' rooms had been cleaned. I opened the bathroom door to find our two black Labrador retrievers immersed in the tub. Upon seeing me, they leapt out, sending Soaky Fun Bubbles everywhere. As my boys and I slipped and slid on the floor, laughing hysterically, I couldn't help but feel sorry for my friend, Marge.

Jackie Fleming

There are times when we envy the orderly, organized life. Focus on the joy of having a full house.

April 24

After five years of enduring the empty arms of childlessness, we waited for Nathan Andrew to arrive. The painful months and years would soon become a dim memory.

A car drove up and parked in front of the house. As a woman stepped out of the car with a blanket-wrapped baby carrier, the scene was suddenly thrown into slow motion, and questions flashed through my mind. What of the girl who had borne him?

I thought of this young girl, 10 years younger than I. She was somewhere in this city, recuperating from the birth of a baby that was no longer hers. After nine months of waiting, she had given life to a little boy. After five years of waiting, we were taking that little boy and giving him the life he deserved. We would be the mother and father who would love him, providing for his physical, emotional and spiritual needs in ways that a young girl was not yet capable of.

With tears in my eyes, I silently thanked a stranger whose baby would become my own. A girl whose gift was a treasure without price.

Sandra Julian

*M*y seven-year-old son, Nicholas, was shot by robbers while we were on vacation in southern Italy. When the doctors told us there was no hope, I wondered how I would ever get through all the years without him. My wife and I did donate his organs to seven very sick Italians, some of whom would certainly be dead by now.

Having been a daily newspaper writer much of my life, I did what comes naturally: I wrote. And wrote. And wrote. And writers all over the world picked up the story from my words and wrote memorable pieces of their own.

In the end, as the words written and spoken about Nicholas found their way around the world, he did more than we could possibly have foreseen. His brief innocent life sent an electric charge through the human spirit, reminding us all of the preciousness of life and hence the importance of living up, rather than down, to it.

Reg Green

Even out of great tragedy
can come some remarkable good.

April 26

It's a chilly Saturday in May, and I'm sitting on a cold metal bench in the stands of a baseball park. I blow on my hands, wishing I'd brought my woolen mittens.

Suddenly, the coach tells me he's starting Matthew in right field. "He's worked hard this year, and I think he deserves the opportunity."

But when the team takes the field, Eddie, the most experienced player, takes right field, and my son is gripping the fence in front of the dugout yelling encouragement.

By the fourth inning, my fingers are stiff and Matthew has been called into the game. Strike one. The next pitch is a ball. Strike two. I cross my fingers. Strike three. My son's head hangs as he walks back to the dugout.

The game ends, and I stretch my legs and try to stomp life back into my feet. While I wait for Matthew, the coach approaches me.

"Mrs. Bodmer, I want you to know that's a fine young man you have there. When I told him he could start, he told me to let Eddie start. That it meant more to him."

I realized then why I sit in the stands. Where else can I watch my son grow into a man?

Judy Bodmer

The way to love anything
is to realize that it may be lost.

G. K. Chesterton

_____

_____

_____

_____

_____

_____

_____

_____

_____

_____

_____

_____

_____

_____

_____

April 28

After 10 months backpacking through Africa and Asia, I was on the final leg of my journey. I looked up at the signs, trying to decipher which train I needed to take to Narita Airport.

Then, out of the masses, a woman stopped and asked, in English, which way I wanted to go. She spoke to the station master in Japanese, found out the platform number, the price of a ticket and the time of departure.

She told me she had been born in Japan, but had spent a year backpacking in New York and knew exactly what it was like to be a woman traveling solo.

She wished me luck, and then she was gone.

Suddenly, she reappeared with a square box wrapped in white and red paper. "For the train. Good-bye." And then she was gone.

As I waited on the platform, my pack didn't feel as heavy. I felt lighter—blessed with the taste of warm food, the dreams of my homecoming and the generosity of a Japanese woman I would know only this once.

Julie Booker

*I*t was in a tiny printing shop on Balboa Island that I first learned women had flown missions in World War II. A customer was making photocopies of a poem called *Celestial Flight* that is read at memorials to women pilots.

"They read this poem at my daughter's funeral," Marilyn said. Her daughter was Captain Candalyn Kubeck. She flew the ValuJet that crashed in the Florida Everglades.

I imagined what this poor mother had gone through, now left behind without a child—a mother who'd had the courage and bravery to let her daughter go into the skies to follow her dream. What could I say to her?

Holding my baby, I could only say good-bye to Captain Candy and to all those other women who took to the skies and are gone. And thanks to all you mothers who let them fly. They didn't reach stardom, but they reached the stars.

Diana L. Chapman

April 30

One day when my son George was eight, he woke up with his foot pointed straight up; he could only walk on his heel. As we began the doctors' circuit, his crookedness moved up one leg and down the other. We learned that he had generalized torsion dystonia, a condition similar to cerebral palsy.

We tried every medication, diet and doctor possible. My life became directed toward helping find a cure for this disease. I wanted my son to be normal again.

Slowly, George's comfort with his disease taught me forgiveness. Then, a friend dragged me to group meditation. I came to realize that George was my teacher; love was the lesson.

I knew then that George was and always had been George. I accepted that he wouldn't grow up and have the same prospects as other people, but he would grow up with more patience, ambition and courage than anyone I had ever known.

At a recent high-school reunion, I listened while everyone celebrated their children's successes. When it was at last my turn, I was the proudest parent: "My son walks. And he's perfect."

Sharon Drew Morgen

*M*rs. Pearson wasn't really a witch, but she lived on our lane in an old gray cottage whose overgrown yard was enclosed by a sagging fence. Every year, at Mother's urging, my sisters and I took one of our handmade May baskets to her house. Our other neighbors always made a great fuss when we visited, but Mrs. Pearson never opened her door.

The year I turned ten we once again crept up to her door, knocked rather halfheartedly and scurried behind a bush. The door slowly opened, and a tiny white-haired lady stepped out. She sat on the top step, our basket in her lap, and suddenly began crying. Ellen, Beth and I climbed the stairs.

"Are you all right?" I asked with concern.

"I just got a bit overwhelmed." Mrs. Pearson invited us in for milk and graham crackers and showed us pictures of her and her sister proudly holding their little paper May baskets.

For the next several years, until we grew too old to weave paper baskets and hide behind lilac bushes, each May Day, we would climb the steps to Mrs. Pearson's porch and find a little basket just for us—full of flower-shaped cookies with pink frosting and sugar sprinkles.

Faith Andrews Bedford

Encourage kindness. It will benefit both the giver and the recipient of the gesture.

May 2

My friend Peggy and I had both been to Paris before, but always as chaperones. This time we wanted to find the real Parisians. One evening we found a tiny café known only to locals. A young woman led us to our seats at the other end of a table already occupied by an elderly couple. She gave us two menus.

For a few minutes, we struggled to recall a few French words. Our tablemates noticed our dilemma. The old man leaned over and explained each dish, one at a time. Since he spoke very little English, his translations took the form of elaborate gestures and animal sounds.

Despite our limited ability to speak the other's language, we continued our lively conversation throughout the meal. We discovered they had been sweethearts for about 10 years. She lived in Paris; he lived in the country. They met once a week to share a pleasant dinner.

Near the end of the evening, a flower vendor made her way through the café. The old gentleman purchased a bouquet, plucked two flowers from the bunch, presented the bouquet to his lady and held out a rose for each of us.

We had found our Paris.

Betty Corbin

had just launched my freelance writing career after working as a political reporter. My mission was to write publishable articles that would find their way into the hearts of magazine editors.

Then the obsession took hold. I was determined to be published in *Los Angeles Magazine*. So, beginner that I was, I marched into the office and asked to see the editor! Nothing doing.

I returned a week later. Still no luck. Now the obsession really took hold, and a wonderful, kooky idea took form. I'd make my friends buy subscriptions to the magazine. So, two days later, armed with 25 checks and my newspaper clips, I marched into the magazine offices. The editor was curious enough to want to meet this obsessed writer, and I left with an assignment.

So, the obsession paid off, and I realized very early in my career that creative marketing and persistence are as important as writing talent.

Frances Halpern

*Determination and perseverance
usually pay big dividends.*

May 4

*You give but little when you give
of your possessions. It is when you give
of yourself that you truly give.*

Kahlil Gibran

_____

_____

_____

_____

_____

_____

_____

_____

_____

_____

_____

_____

_____

_____

_____

_____

Ma

*W*hen I was in my middle-school years, parents' property had a huge, old oak ti in a secluded corner that I'd climb. I'd sit there, fantasizi about this or that, or camp out for a good long cry whe things were particularly melodramatic.

On one particularly tough day, I grabbed my notebook out of my backpack and started writing a poem about the feelings I was experiencing.

The writing calmed me, setting free the harmful thoughts that had had me in their grip. The next afternoon, I went straight to my tree, wanting to see if what had worked once would work again. What began that long-ago afternoon was to become a lifelong love affair with words.

When I put thought on paper today, whether it be for a particularly compelling piece of fiction or a more mundane news piece, there is always the memory of that first thrill of capturing each moment as it happens, of knowing that, no matter how far distant it becomes in memory, the simple act of writing will keep it forever safe, forever authentic.

Kate M. Brausen

May 6

Children are little hoarders at heart and are seldom interested in sharing. They see. They want. They keep.

The other day my five-year-old daughter brought out her supply of comic books.

"This is mine and this is mine and this is mine and ..."

"Wait a minute," my wife said. "That one isn't yours. That's Richard's. It's got his name written on top."

The evidence wasn't accepted.

"You have to give it back to Richard," my wife countered.

"No."

Then followed a long discourse on the rights of others, the many advantages of being honest, the promise of dire consequences if Jane didn't cough up the comic book.

"Now, whose book is that?" my wife asked.

"Richard's," Jane answered sullenly.

Richard was then summoned from the backyard. "Here's your comic book, Richard," Jane said.

"I don't want it," Richard replied, running off to rejoin his pals.

Gary Lautens

*W*hen the British Tourist Authority invited me to tour England, I asked my two best friends on the travel magazine staff to go with me. Linda, Leslie and I are city girls, born and bred, so we were not prepared when our tour guide instructed us on the fine art of flipping sheep.

"At this time of year," she explained, "their coats get very heavy, and they begin to itch, so they roll on the ground to scratch their backs. Then they're too heavy to get back up. If you see a sheep on her back with her feet in the air, you'll need to go into the pasture and set her back on her feet. You also have to wait until her organs slip back into place and her brain settles in her head again."

Back in our cottage, after a day of touring, we sat in front of our fireplace. Linda was sprawled out on the couch.

"Linda," Leslie said, "are you asleep?"

Linda opened one eye. "Go practice on Phyllis. She's got a heavier coat."

I glowered. "Only one of you may be going on the next trip!"

Linda looked at Leslie. "I'll flip you for it."

Phyllis W. Zeno

Take your sense of humor
with you, wherever you go.

May 8

At the age of 15, Lee Katherine had dreams of becoming a marine biologist. It was at this time that she was diagnosed with cancer of the nasal cavity. Although her parents did everything they could to help her fight her illness, her medical team soon realized that Lee Katherine was losing her battle.

"Mom, there is one thing I want to do before I die. I want to swim with dolphins."

Ruth called the Children's Wish Foundation International, and that very day plans were set into motion to transport Lee Katherine from North Carolina to the Florida Keys.

What happened was a miracle to all who were present. Two dolphins seemed to sense her fragile condition. They nudged her neck, gave her soft dolphin kisses, provided gentle piggyback rides.

After her swim, Lee Katherine told her parents, "I'm not afraid to die anymore." The communication with the dolphins was her "bridge to the other side," and she was totally peaceful. Just 36 hours after her swim, Lee Katherine passed away, and her parents fulfilled their daughter's final wish. They scattered her ashes amongst the same school of dolphins that had been her "bridge to the other side."

Christy Chappelear Andrews

*Many people will walk in and out of your life.
But only true friends will leave
footprints in your heart.*

Eleanor Roosevelt

_____

_____

_____

_____

_____

_____

_____

_____

_____

_____

_____

_____

_____

_____

May 10

When my husband and I decided it was time to think about having a baby, I never dreamed it would be a 10-year venture. Fertility drugs coupled with artificial insemination failed. Our first try with in vitro fertilization ended with my miscarrying twins. After two more unsuccessful attempts at IVF, I needed a break.

My husband and I settled into a life of two working professionals. In the meantime, some very dear friends had their second baby. Since they didn't intend to have any more children, Kathy offered to carry a baby for us if we got to the point where we considered using a gestational carrier.

After six more unsuccessful IVF attempts, we began the process of having my frozen embryos sent to a fertility clinic near Kathy. Insurance regulations also required that two embryos of the 10 or 12 retrieved be implanted in the real mother.

While we awaited news from Kathy, we learned the results of my pregnancy test. The price we had paid through our prolonged trial resulted in the birth of beautiful, healthy Benjamin George Cameransi III.

Patricia K. Cameransi

***Children are miracles no matter how
they find their way into your heart.***

*S*ean Eric Fox entered the world weighing just one pound, seven ounces. When I saw him for the first time, I was filled with despair. He had lobster-red skin, his eyes were closed, and he had so many tubes that I couldn't find a place on his body to touch. I tried to carry on as if everything was okay. I was afraid I might have to tell Samantha and Emma that their brother might never come home. As I sat by his incubator, my heart pounded each time a monitor went off signaling his oxygen level had dropped. I wept when doctors said he needed surgery. But no matter how high his fever raged or how much pain he was in, Sean never gave up. Brushing away a tear, I thought, *If a six-week-old preemie can fight that hard, why can't I?* And though I wasn't sure how, I knew that I had to be more like Sean.

As if Sean sensed my renewed spirit, he seemed to fight even harder, and after 12 weeks, he finally came home. I'll always be inspired by the fighting spirit that saw him through those first hard days—and taught me everything I know about courage and hope.

Ami Fox as told to Dianne Gill

May 12

I've spent most of my career as a traveling salesman. One year my five-year-old daughter pressed a gift into my hands. It was a stuffed toy penguin, and attached to its right wing was a tiny, wooden sign with a hand-painted declaration: "I Love My Dad!"

After that day, she always helped me pack and saw to it that the penguin went in along with my socks and shaving kit. That little penguin has traveled hundreds of thousands of miles. And we have made many friends along the way.

Late one night, after driving over a hundred miles from my previous hotel, I unpacked only to discover that the penguin was missing. Frantically, I phoned the hotel. My penguin had been found.

Jeanine is in college now, and I don't travel as much anymore. The penguin spends most of its time sitting on my dresser—a reminder that love is the best traveling companion.

Edmund W. Boyle

*O*ne Sunday afternoon, my six-year-old daughter queried from the video closet, "Mommy, where are my Barney videos?" I reminded her that a few months earlier she had let friends borrow the videos for their recently adopted child.

Remembering the loan, she returned disappointed to the video closet to make an alternate decision. She came to my side two minutes later and, with big, brown-eyed child wisdom, said, "Don't you just sometimes wish you could rewind life?"

Yes. There are some special moments and milestones that I would love to relive, choices I would make differently, and embarrassing moments I would gladly rescind. But as you stand beside me as a continuous source of pride and great joy, and evolve each day into a beautiful young lady, I want to reach for the "VCR of Life" and put you on pause!

Beverley Bolger Gordon

Sometimes we wish we could go back and relive moments, but watching the future unfold is much better.

May 14

*There are times when parenthood seems like
nothing but feeding the mouth that bites you.*

Peter DeVries

*I*n 1994, I was on top of the world. I had just signed the largest contract in the history of the retail service industry! I had just turned 40; I had two healthy, happy sons; we were buying the house of our dreams. And then I found a lump in my breast.

Four weeks after my surgery, I awoke in the middle of the night with a vision: cartoons. I made my way to my desk, and 50 cancer-related cartoons started flowing into my head. I scribbled madly, sketching and writing, until I was exhausted.

My cartoons and "my book" became my focus as I searched for signs of humor in my treatments. The harder I looked, the more I found, and my first book, *Not Now ... I'm Having a No Hair Day!* was born. Exactly one year from the day I sat in the hospital recovering from cancer surgery, I sat in my publisher's office and signed a contract for two books about using humor as a tool to deal with a diagnosis of cancer.

Christine Clifford

With the right attitude, you can turn your darkest hour into your life's work.

May 16

Through the years I often heard my mother say: "When a kid's in trouble, close your mouth and open your arms." I tried to follow that advice while my own were growing up, but with five children in six years, I didn't always succeed.

When my children were teens, they gave me many more opportunities to practice Mom's wisdom, but I'll confess that advice wasn't the first thing that came to mind when a teacher or principal called.

Yet on the occasions when I remembered Mom's technique, I didn't have to retract biting sarcasm or apologize for false assumptions or rescind unrealistic punishments. When I held my tongue, I also heard about their fears, anger, guilt and repentance. They didn't get defensive because I wasn't accusing.

One of my grown children came to me a few months back. "Mom, I did a stupid thing. . . ."

I listened for nearly an hour while she sifted through the dilemma. When we stood up, I got a bear hug and heard "Thanks, Mom. I knew you'd help me solve this."

It's amazing how smart I sound when I close my mouth and open my arms.

Diane C. Perrone

Whenever a child's in trouble,
close your mouth and open your arms.

As far back as I can remember, the large pickle jar sat on the floor beside the dresser in my parents' bedroom. When Dad got ready for bed, he would empty his pockets and toss his coins into the jar. When the jar was filled, Dad would roll the coins and take them to the bank. As he slid the rolled coins across the counter at the bank, he would grin proudly. "These are for my son's college fund. He'll never work at the mill all his life like me."

The years passed, and I finished college and took a job in another town. On a visit home, I noticed that the pickle jar had been removed. It had served its purpose.

When I married, I told my wife about the pickle jar. The first Christmas after our daughter was born, we spent the holiday with my parents. After dinner my wife took the baby into my parents' bedroom to diaper her.

When she came back, she took my hand and led me into the room. To my amazement, there, as if it had never been removed, stood the old pickle jar, the bottom already covered with coins.

A. W. Cobb

Every little penny, carefully saved, can shape a future.

May 18

I distinctly remember the May Day of the year I was in fifth grade. Pam, one of my dearest friends, was a year older than I, and her interests were starting to change from those we had shared together. I felt hurt and left out.

When my mother asked if I was going to take a basket to Pam, I responded angrily, "Absolutely not!"

My mom stopped what she was doing and explained that one of the greatest things friends can do is to give each other a chance to grow, change and develop. And sometimes that would mean choosing to spend time with other people.

It was hard, but I decided to forgive Pam and express that forgiveness by giving her a May Day basket. "Thank you, Susie," she said, scooping up the flowers. "I hoped you wouldn't forget me!"

That day changed my life. I decided to hold my friends tightly in my heart, but loosely in my expectations of them, allowing them space to grow and to change—with or without me.

Sue Dunigan

"*D*o you know how to type?" Dick Bauer asked me outside the Des Plaines Theater. "Because if you can, go over to the *Suburban Times* office before four. They need somebody to write the high-school sports for the paper."

I peddled across town to talk with Floyd Fulle. "Fill up the page and have it here Tuesday morning before school. If you can type, it's ten dollars a week."

Getting information was simple enough. Everybody liked to talk about themselves. I wrote two articles in one afternoon. All that was missing was putting the text and the schedules into typed form.

My dad had brought home a typewriter that I suspect he'd paid three dollars for someone to pull out of some storage bin. I began at about five and started the hunt for letters. No "e." At 5:15 the next morning, I had finished typing and handwrote in the "e's."

That afternoon I called Floyd Fulle. "Get the 'e' on the typewriter fixed. Don't use the word 'and' so often. Get your check every Tuesday morning."

I was a journalist!

Gordon Burgett

Don't be afraid to take chances.
Success follows those who take risks.

May 20

*W*hen I was pregnant with our second child and nearing the end of my term, it became quite obvious that my husband's waistline had begun to rival mine.

One morning while standing in the kitchen with our then three-year-old daughter, we noticed that she had begun to eye us curiously. Though she had been frequently schooled about the arrival of her new baby sister, something seemed to confuse her. Courtney looked at her father, then looked at me. Again she returned her gaze to her father. Thoughtfully, and with all the seriousness a three-year-old could muster, she asked, "Daddy, when are you going to have YOUR baby?"

Laurin Broadbent

Who is it that loves me and will love me forever with an affection which no chance, no misery, no crime of mine can do away? It is you, my mother.

Thomas Carlyle

_____

_____

_____

_____

_____

_____

_____

_____

_____

_____

_____

_____

_____

_____

_____

May 22

James and Pamela are my husband's children. Shortly after I met my husband, his children came for a visit that lasted for two weeks and then for the summer. For a variety of reasons, their mother never returned for them. I can't say I was thrilled. I had not wanted children of my own, and raising someone else's did not appeal to me. The kids weren't crazy about the idea either.

Carl and I married Christmas day, and shortly after the wedding James and I cleared up the mommy issue once and for all. It was his fourth birthday, and I had taken the children to the grocery store to get a few things for the party. He was talking a mile a minute and said one word that immediately caught my attention. "I called you Mommy," he giggled. "I'm sorry." James twisted his mouth a bit.

"You don't have to be sorry. You have your mother, and she is your mommy. I am whatever you want me to be."

James was telling me in his own wonderful way that I am not raising someone else's children—I am raising my children.

Trudy Bowler

taught in the same fourth-grade classroom where I was once a student. The first day of school usually brought no surprises, but this year was different.

Danny had moved from Kentucky. His dad was a truck driver, and his mom worked odd jobs to help make ends meet.

In October I put Danny's name on the mitten and hat list. He was so proud when he received them.

He wasn't a very good student, but he was a remarkable artist, so I incorporated art projects into the reading curriculum to boost his self-esteem.

When it came time for the Christmas gift exchange, I knew I would need to help with his gift as I had done for other students. The room mothers collected a quarter from each child who could afford it and bought a present for me.

The day of the party was exciting. After everyone left for the day, I went to straighten my desk. I found a folded piece of construction paper. It was a note that said, "To my favorite teacher. I couldn't afford to get you anything, so I am giving you everything I have. Love, Danny."

Inside was taped a dime.

Karen Wasmer

May 24

When a tornado touched down in a small town nearby, many families were left devastated. One Sunday, I taped a picture of a young family to our refrigerator, explaining their plight to my seven-year-old twin boys and to three-year-old Meghan. I brought three large boxes into the living room. I encouraged the boys to go through their toys and donate some of their less favorite things. "I'll help you find something for the little girl when I'm done with this," I said to Meghan.

As I filled the third box, Meghan walked up with her much-loved rag doll. "Lucy makes me happy, Mommy. Maybe she'll make that other little girl happy, too."

I suddenly realized that anyone can give their castoffs away. True generosity is giving that which you cherish most.

I, who had wanted to teach, had been taught.

Elizabeth Cobb

True generosity is not giving your castoffs, but giving up the things you cherish most.

*A*t the age of 55, I became an "overnight" success. My first novel, *Power of One*, was sold for a million dollars and printed in 11 languages. I had written seriously every day of my life since the age of 11. Instead of being an overnight success, I was, in effect, a pathetically slow learner.

But I got there in the end because I learned that writing is about time and practice. It is about time spent with words until eventually they become your friends and begin to cooperate with your gifted storyteller's mind. Until you have written at least three hours a day, or 15 hours a working week, you will not sufficiently master the craft of words to be effective as a writer.

And the single most important ingredient in becoming a published author? Bum glue. Glue your bum to a chair and keep going, and never give up.

Bryce Courtenay

Success is about being the most determined, about hanging on the longest and never giving up.

May 26

As a novice grandma, I eagerly looked forward to the first time I'd hear, "Mom, can you keep the baby a couple of days?"

The calendar was cleared, crib set up in the guest room, and friends were put on alert that I would be holding open house for the debut of our little princess.

What a joyful experience, that first grandchild. She had added a dimension to life impossible to measure or explain. And all her father's sins, from colic to wrecking the family car, were forgiven.

The second night, Baby decided to see how quickly Grandma could get to her crib when she called. Grandma hit the floor running each time. She remained happy and content for the rest of our time until five minutes before her parents walked in the front door. They found me, hair stringing, shirttail out, walking the floor and crooning. I never convinced them that Baby hadn't done that for two days.

But I had passed my maiden grandbaby-sitting test, and they did let me do it again. By the time I was rocking my seventh baby grand, my beginner's luck had seasoned to old pro status.

Billie B. Chesney

May 27

My son, an Air Force career man, was sent to Turkey when my grandson was six months old. "He won't know me when you get back to the States," I said brokenly at the airport. As the weeks passed, I was determined to find a way to forge a bond between my grandson and me.

I bought a children's picture book, a blank cassette tape and a disposable camera. I recorded me reading the book, and when I finished the story, I spoke a few words to Damon, ending with, "Always remember that Grandma loves you very much." I had friends take snapshots of me doing routine grandmotherly things, including reading the book. I sent the package to my son and his wife.

Every few months, Damon would receive a new story package from Grandma. Three years later, at the airport, Damon saw me first. Breaking away from my daughter-in-law, he ran toward me, crying out, "It's Grandma! You're my Grandma!"

I would never, ever tire of hearing that word.

Ruth Ayers

May 28

On one of my numerous visits to the remote Fijian island of Taveuni, I met a man named Joe. Joe built bures, traditional thatched houses. The fact that he moved slowly was never to be mistaken for a sign of age, for on Taveuni, even spry youngsters moved slowly most of the time.

"Building a good bure takes a lot of resting," Joe said. During those rest periods, Joe often asked me questions about other places.

One afternoon, Joe noticed the daytime moon and said, with some authority, "Did you know the Americans have been to the moon? The moon is a long way from here, isn't it? It must have taken them a long time to get there."

He was talking about it as if it happened quite recently, so I felt compelled to tell him that the first moon landing had happened almost 30 years ago and that they had been back several times since.

Joe turned to me and said sincerely and with a smile, "Well, there couldn't have been much to see on the moon because I heard about it only last week."

Rob Bundy

Look at what you think is important through someone else's eyes. It can help you reevaluate priorities.

Nothing in life is to be feared.
It is only to be understood.

Madame Curie

_____

_____

_____

_____

_____

_____

_____

_____

_____

_____

_____

_____

_____

_____

_____

_____

May 30

On September 13, 2002, we stood in front of a World War I monument in Bradley Beach, New Jersey. We came in honor of those who perished and those who survived September 11, 2001. We lit candles and cried together and shared stories about the day and how it affected us.

Later, when the memorial service was over, the children left the park to stand on the corner. Suddenly, we noticed horns honking up and down Main Street, as if there was a celebration.

We couldn't imagine who would celebrate on a day like today. Then we heard the children's chants. "Beep if you love America!" they shouted, again and again. And everyone did. The night air was filled with horns honking and people waving as the children jumped in the air, holding flags in front of them and shouting.

That night, for a while, we let the children lead and heal us.

"Beep if you love America," we roared.

And we knew America would hear us.

Harriet May Savitz

signed up as a journalism major in college only to be told by my professor that he wasn't sure I'd be able to make the grade. I had failed the entrance exam on English and was put in the "bonehead" English class. That made me a loser. I promised myself I'd work three times as hard to prove him wrong. When I graduated with my journalism degree, I went to work on a small paper and then was drafted. After my army stint, I did what was necessary to support my family, but something kept driving me on to become a novelist.

I decided to specialize and began to read and analyze Western novels. Gradually I learned what a plot was, how characters interacted and how a story could be plot-driven or character-driven. I'll never forget the day my first book sold; soon I had created a series.

By now I've had 286 books (both fiction and non-fiction) published. I'm not sure if I ever would have become a writer if it hadn't been for that professor who said I probably couldn't make the grade.

Chet Cunningham

Being told you can't do something motivates you to prove them wrong.

June 1

By the time we discovered the dinner plate's flaw—a small bulge on the bottom that caused it to spin freely—the packaging and receipt had long been discarded. Even though it was one of eight, and there were only four of us, it turned up on the table with annoying regularity. We began to devise sneaky ways of avoiding ending up with the dreaded Spinner Plate.

Then my husband decided one evening to at least compensate the plate's unlucky recipient each time it came into use. "From now on," he announced, "anyone caught with the Spinner Plate will receive extra kisses." He then turned to our daughter and kissed her heartily all over both cheeks. He invited our son and I to do the same. Our daughter felt special, and it was the beginning of a complete about-face in our attitudes toward the Spinner Plate.

The children still tried to manipulate the plate's position, but for a different reason. And if one of the family had a particularly trying day, the Spinner Plate was purposely set at his or her place. After a round of kisses, dinner would begin with troubles eased.

Lori Broadfoot

*F*atigue has a variety of causes, most of which begin at the moment of conception and continue through the childrearing years. What's worse, even after our children have grown, they will continue to make us tired. They will find us in our houseboats off the deserted islands we purchase with our 401(k) money. It will not matter that we left no forwarding address. There they will be, and most likely, they will have reproduced.

Of some comfort is that most mothers find they are able to secure employment, maintain a semi-efficient household, meet the basic needs of their children, create a Caesar Augustus costume in 24 minutes and still carry on an adult conversation.

Fatigue, as mothers know and accept, is nothing more than the tradeoff for the pleasure of kissing your son's jam-smeared face; for being the one he wants when he is sick; for hearing his teacher say, "He's a great kid." Fatigue is the small price we pay for being our child's safe harbor—for his whisper in the dark, "Can I sleep in your bed?"

Staci Ann Richmond

June 3

I was in my midthirties and a professional writer when I decided I would like to go to college. With five children to educate, my husband asked, "Where is the money coming from?"

The answer was deceptively simple: "I'll sell the things I learn."

Our deal was, I would enroll part-time, but if I could not put myself through college by marketing the knowledge gained from my classes, I would drop out.

I made my first major sale during Psychology 101, when we were training rats to run through mazes. I sold an article showing how these techniques could be applied to one's own children for enough money to cover a full semester's tuition.

Journalism courses, especially those in news photography, were lucrative, and English classes also proved fruitful.

On graduation day, I pecked out an essay called "A Graduate in the Family"; my husband snapped a photo. The article sold, and both my husband and I got paid.

College proved quite profitable. My writing income actually tripled immediately, and, in the years since then, has gone far beyond that.

Lois Duncan

"*L*ook, Mom, the tooth fairy left me twenty-five cents!"

We chatted for a few minutes, then he said, "Is there really a tooth fairy, or do you put this money in my tooth pillow and take away my tooth?"

"What would you like to think, Simon?" I asked, stalling for time.

"It doesn't really matter," he said with confidence. "If there is a tooth fairy, that's pretty exciting, and if it's you, that's pretty nice, too."

I concluded that no disappointment would result from my answer, so I confessed to being his benefactor. Then I cautioned him not to say anything to his younger brother, explaining, "Each child is entitled to the magic until he or she is ready. Do you understand?"

"Yes," he said nodding, "but one more question, Mom. Does Dad know?"

Elaine Decker

Find the right moment to let children in on the secrets of life.

June 5

I was blessed with three beautiful, intelligent and terrific children, who are now 30, 29 and 28. But at one point they were seven, six and five.

My youngest daughter came home from kindergarten one day and asked, "Mommy, how many children did you want?"

Thinking for a minute, I looked at her and said, "Two."

She thought about it for a moment and then asked, "Me, and who else?"

Kathrine A. Barhydt

There is nothing like a child's self-esteem.

Life is a flame that is always burning itself out,
but it catches fire again every time
a child is born.

George Bernard Shaw

June 7

When my husband, Allen, called to tell me that finally a baby might be available for us to adopt, we wasted no time filling out the applications and telling the birth mother why we would make good parents. Several weeks went by with no word, and then months, and I pondered what might have been. In December I received an unexpected phone call from the attorney handling the case. "The girl is back in town, and she has selected you and Allen." And so the countdown began.

Little by little I began to think like a mother. Our request for a family health history from the birth mother led a series of notes between us that eventually shifted away from discussions of health. And, oddly enough, this stranger turned into a friend.

Falling in love with our baby girl came naturally, but when Allen and I decided to adopt, I did not expect to feel love for a stranger. In the hospital's gift bag, I saw the final letter from my friend. Her love-filled note ended, "I gave her life, now you give her love."

Debra Ayers Brown

There are no courses in how to be a best friend, or in how to find one either. The prerequisites for friendship are nonstop talking at the same time for at least seven and a half hours, followed by going home and then calling each other on the phone to discuss all the things that were not discussed in person.

My best friend, Judith, is a columnist, like me. Her refrigerator art is identical to mine, her husband is acceptable and, most important of all, she has a generous spirit, meaning she is not petty or jealous.

I recently called Judith and asked her what her Thanksgiving column was about.

"It's about how every time I look at jellied cranberry sauce, I think it must be the stuff that they vacuum out during liposuction."

But my column is about her. And now I have to pencil seven and a half hours into my schedule so we can talk about it. The screaming alone should take four and a half.

Stephanie Brush

**Finding a best friend, or being one,
is no easy task.**

June 9

"ommy, when are you gonna be a writer?" my six-year-old asked me.

"Uh, Jeffrey, what do I have to do to be a writer?"

"Write a book for me and my friends. Will you do that, Mommy?"

The next day, Jeff announced he had told everybody at school I was going to write a book and we could put it in the library. Suddenly, I realized that this project was not going to go away. So I wrote the book. I rewrote it and rewrote it again.

Finally, after four years, numerous rewrites and numerous rejections, my children's book was actually published. Although Jeff was now in sixth grade, the book's dedication read, "To Jeff Fields, who always believed this book would come to be."

And five years after Jeff had first requested a book, we had an official ceremony in the school library.

Terri Fields

Starting a project is the easy part.
Following it through to completion
takes the time.

*K*evin came running from one end of the house to the other, screaming with the telephone in his hand, "It's Santa, Mom! He's called our house!"

I took the phone and said, "Hello?"

I heard my friend Sandra, laughing, "All I said was, 'Hi, Kevin, it's Sandra!'"

I was about to speak when I caught the sparkle in Kevin's eye. I smiled into the phone and spoke: "Yes, Santa, Kevin and Sean have been really good boys. It was so nice of you to phone. Thank you."

I paused a moment as there was silence on the other end of the line. "And Merry Christmas to you, too, Santa," and I gently hung up the receiver.

Kittie Ellis

Take time to keep children's dreams alive.

June 11

I was once asked by the Americans to write how, when I die, I want to be remembered.

What really matters is that I do bring happiness to people, for the simple reason that my heroines are the sweet, loving, genuine women who were first portrayed by Shakespeare in *Romeo and Juliet* and whose example has been copied by all classical authors.

It is they who evoke in a man the real love that is both spiritual and physical, and it is the woman in a marriage who stands for Morality, Compassion, Sympathy and Love.

Dame Barbara Cartland

June 12

Last December, Justin Nebe finished his high-school coursework. In February he attended boot camp. In May, he graduated from boot camp and attended his high-school graduation in his Marine uniform.

Being the first Marine in his family makes Justin Nebe proud. His parents say it makes them proud, too, but now they are fearful, too.

Dressed in his uniform, Justin moves differently. When he leaves this time, he and his family do not know when they will see each other again. Justin has already said good-bye to his father and his sister. An assembly line soon forms, and his mother, grandmother and a friend take the bags as they are packed and place them in the foyer.

He hugs his mother and his grandmother. Mrs. Nebe isn't quite ready to let go. Tears are slipping down her cheeks. "Do you have your wallet? All your money?" Justin finally gets into his friend's truck and leans out the passenger window. "Bye. Love you guys," he says. And the truck roars away.

Karen A. Thomas

June 13

I stared at the stick in disbelief. Two straight pink lines. I was seized by fear.

I'm close to 30 years old, but my complexion is 16. Nausea is my constant companion, and my bladder has shrunk to the size of a lima bean. My husband assured me the only thing hysterical about this pregnancy is me.

And my maternity underwear.

But I have to say, the most amazing transformation is how neurotic I've become about this little person who isn't even born yet. Our baby.

When I saw the first sonogram of our baby, I saw a little girl taking her first steps, walking to school, getting her driver's license, going to college, getting married, having babies of her own. I also wondered how I could possibly protect her from all the bad waiting out there for her, while letting her experience the good.

In that instant I realized there are much scarier things than shapeless maternity underwear. But you know what? I'm ready.

Kristen Cook

*If one advances confidently in the direction
of his dreams and endeavors to live the life
which he has imagined, he will meet
with success unexpected in common hours.*

Henry David Thoreau

_____

_____

_____

_____

_____

_____

_____

_____

_____

_____

_____

_____

_____

_____

_____

June 15

Papa believed that the greatest sin of which we were capable was to go to bed at night as ignorant as we had been when we had awakened that day. So he devised a ritual. At dinner we would share what new things we had learned that day. If we had nothing to share, we didn't dare sit at the table without first finding a fact in our much-used encyclopedia.

As children, we thought very little about how we were being enriched. "How long we live is limited," Papa said, "but how much we learn is not. What we learn is what we are. No one should miss out on an education."

Now, when I get home, before my head hits the pillow, I hear Papa's voice resound clearly in my room. "Felice," he asks, "what did you learn today?" If I can't recall even one new thing, I get out of bed and scan the bookshelves to find something. Then with that accomplished, Papa and I can rest soundly, assured that a day has not been wasted.

Leo Buscaglia

The greatest sin is to go to bed at night as ignorant as we were when we woke up that day.

*A*nnette, pregnant and showing, and I, with my hurt knee, decided to take our kids and get away. We packed the van carefully. With five children under the age of seven, we knew our trip would not be lacking adventure.

Before long, our crew became restless.

"Hey," Annette said in her teacher voice, "half the fun is getting there!"

Soon we stood on the doorsteps of my parents' mountain home.

"Who's got the key?" one of the kids hollered.

Oh, no! I had left the key on my kitchen counter. Quickly turning our situation into a game, Annette, the kids and I looked for a way inside. We found a window that didn't have a safety lock, and I hoisted Janet up so she could crawl through. As her feet disappeared, one of the kids shouted, "Mom, remember that half the fun is getting there!"

Janet Lynn Mitchell

June 17

One day, I realized with sudden clarity that something was missing from my life. I'd raised two children and progressed from secretary to vice president over many careers, but doing more of what I was doing and getting more of what I was getting wasn't going to fill the void.

I found myself inexplicably drawn to a "Retire in Mexico" conference, and on my flight to Guadalajara, I sat next to an extraordinary Mexican woman. After we had talked awhile, Iona withdrew a velvet-wrapped package from her straw bag. "Do you know tarot?" she asked. Though not much of a believer in mystical phenomena, I agreed to let her read for me.

I leaned back and closed my eyes. Then, unbidden, a little voice within me whispered, "Listen."

Shortly after our encounter, I left behind my spreadsheets and security, trusting those synchronistic signs planted in front of me, and moved to a wonderful, cobblestoned village in Mexico. That voice inside me is my little artist who has been responsible for my publishing a book. She's taught me to reprioritize my values, give back to the community and discover my own spirituality—and to discover what was missing in my life. Wholeness.

Karen Blue

**If something is missing in your life,
follow the voice inside you.**

June 18

I was 16 years old when my mother began writing her murder mystery/romance novel. Tragically, she got sick and died before she could submit her manuscript. It was willed to me, and I put it in my closet where it remained for eight years.

The birth of my son pushed me to my mother's manuscript. I felt a link to my past, present and future, and I ached for my mother.

Everyone in the field discouraged my submitting it. Reason: There could be no second novel. But I had it photocopied and decided to submit it anyway.

In the middle of a hectic day, the doorbell rang. Doubleday wanted the book. Then came the ordeal of having to tell the editor there would be no second book. "I still want the book," she said. And so *Living Image* was published, and my mother, who had given both love and life to me, was able to get a touch of immortality.

Pat Gallant

Always finish unfinished business.

June 19

*W*hen my high-school home-economics teacher announced that we would be having a formal mother-daughter tea, I felt certain I would not be serving my mother at this special event.

Who would be looking after Granny who was bedridden following a stroke? Who would be home to greet my three little sisters when they got home from school? How would she get here, since we didn't own a car and she couldn't afford a taxi?

So I will never forget walking into the gaily decorated gym—and there she was, wearing a red dress with tiny white flowers, just right for the tea.

I was so proud! I served her tea and introduced her boldly to the group. The look of love in her eyes told me she understood how important it was to me.

One of the promises I made to myself and to my children was that I would always be there for them. That promise is sometimes difficult to keep, but I have an example before me that puts any lame excuses to rest. I just recall when Mother came to tea.

Margie M. Coburn

June 20

*M*y stepchildren hadn't asked to live with their father and me. I could feel how much they missed their "other mother," but some days I didn't want them around, a feeling I was too ashamed to admit having. We needed to find the boundaries of our new relationship, and it was through my own daughter that I finally learned to be a stepmom.

Suddenly, she had a brother and a sister. Not a step-brother or half-sister. And was there really any other way to see it?

Soon the everyday motions of life took over. We began to fill the photo albums and create memories. I took my daughters door-to-door selling Girl Scout cookies. I walked the windy streets on Halloween.

When you get right down to the nitty-gritty, to the dirty laundry and the scabbed knees, there really isn't any difference between a stepmom and a natural mom. What's important is that there is a mom who loves and cares.

Janie Emaus

June 21

Opportunity . . . often it comes in the form of misfortune, or temporary defeat.

Napoleon Hill

_____
_____
_____
_____
_____
_____
_____
_____
_____
_____
_____
_____
_____
_____
_____
_____

had wanted to try my hand at selling my writing for a long time, but I wouldn't even try. Fear and doubts had blocked me. I was in my seventh year as an athletic coach when I finally mustered enough courage to sign up for a "Writing and Selling Magazine Articles" class.

A few weeks into it, I was challenged to write a query letter to read to the class. I was shocked when the instructor said, "It's ready. Fire it off to the magazine."

My second shock came when I was commissioned to write an article. I had finally made it; I was now a published writer.

Adrenaline flowed as I wrote and sold 14 articles. But then my first of many rejections caught me off guard, my confidence began to wane, and I put my writing aside. I let fear keep me from writing for 10 years and became a top-notch teacher instead.

Until I decided to try writing again. I began selling right away.

I'm glad I faced my fears and began writing. Otherwise, I would have led a pretty boring life. And I've even gained a bit of confidence along the way.

Bud Gardner

Not facing your fears and overcoming them can lead to a boring life.

June 23

*A*fter a last-ditch attempt at a hospital stay, my husband and I had to make plans for our daughter's future that did not include bringing her home. "Your daughter is depressed and suicidal," a psychiatric consultant said. "May I suggest a wonderful environment for her in northern Idaho?"

For five months her father and I did not hear from Lara. Then a letter arrived thanking us for her new clothes. The communication got better, and that led to our first visit. Each time we came, we saw more improvement.

Two and a half years flew by as Lara bloomed like a rose, my husband and I became one again, and our son became happy and self-confident. I think we were meant to go through all this pain, for only when one experiences such pain can one experience such joy.

Eventually Lara graduated from U. C. Irvine with honors and was accepted as the youngest member of the San Francisco Opera Company.

For those struggling with children with problems, don't give up. There is a light at the end of the tunnel. We know. We have been there.

Bobbi Bisserier

When there appears to be no hope, don't give up. There is a light at the end of the tunnel.

$\mathcal{M}$y husband and I had been together for six years, and with him I had watched as his young children became young teenagers. When the children moved to a town five hours away, we promptly set up an e-mail and chat-line service.

Late one evening, as my husband snoozed and I was catching up on my e-mail, an "instant message" from Margo, my oldest stepdaughter, appeared on the screen. As we had done in the past, we sent several messages back and forth, exchanging the latest news. That night she didn't ask if it was me or her dad on the other end of the keyboard, and I didn't identify myself either. After a while I commented that it was late and I should get to sleep. The return message read, "Okay, talk to you later! Love you!"

A wave of sadness ran through me, and I realized that she must have thought she was writing to her father. I simply responded, "Love you, too! Have a good sleep!"

Then, Margo's final message appeared: "Tell Dad good night for me, too."

Judy E. Carter

June 25

In 1966, Tupperware parties were all the rage with stay-at-home moms. These parties gave us a pleasant and acceptable way to go out for the evening and actually talk with people older than five. One day, my friend Kay, who lived two doors down from me, yelled over the back fence that she had some pastries left over and maybe we should gather up some neighbors and finish them off with coffee. This was an unusual idea in our neighborhood.

This time we decided to forego the kids' naps for once and let them play while we talked. Something happened that afternoon that we all knew we wanted to continue.

We met every Friday afternoon for three more years—bringing the kids along to scatter toys and grind pretzels into the dining-room rug of whoever was hosting that week. We didn't mind the mess. We were learning we weren't alone in the world. Week by week, my sanity was saved and my marriage was strengthened because I found a safe place to vent my frustrations and learn new ways of coping.

Who knew Tupperware could preserve so many things!

Carol Bryant

Mothers getting together and talking learn they aren't alone in the world.

*O*h, those dreaded words! But here was my trusted, very best friend telling me she was fixing me up on a blind date. We were juniors in high school and had been best friends since first grade. She must have been crazy thinking she was going to fix me up with her boyfriend's friend. And going to Disneyland where I would be stuck with some strange geek for hours and hours.

Sue and I had a huge fight. Back and forth we argued. I decided to talk to my mother who I knew would be on my side and back me up.

My mother said, "You're just going to Disneyland—you're not going to marry the guy!"

Famous last words! Four years later, I did marry that very guy! And now, some 30 years later, my blind date, our three sons and I still tease my mother about her famous last words. And I am still the very best of friends with Sue. Who knew it would turn out the way it did? Thanks, Sue.

Barbara LoMonaco

June 27

When Martin Wall was released from a prison camp in Siberia, he received word that his family was dead. Slowly he began to regain his health and strength, but his heart was dead.

Then, one morning, he met Greta. Life became worth living again, and soon they were married. Greta longed for children, but she never became pregnant.

On her day off, Greta headed to an orphanage to find a child. A little girl smiled shyly at her, and Greta asked, "Would you like to come home with me to a real home?"

"Oh, yes," she replied, "but I have to stay with my brother."

Greta pleaded with Martin. Finally, he suggested they both return. Martin was instantly drawn to the frail, thin boy who held the hand of the wide-eyed little girl. "We will take them both," he said.

When Greta arrived at the desk, she found Martin in a daze. "Greta, read the names!" Taking the paper she read: Jacob and Sonya Wall, mother Anna (Bartel) Wall. Father, Martin Wall."

"Oh, Greta, this is my beloved son Jacob and the daughter I never knew I had! This is a miracle!"

Elizabeth Enns

Believe in miracles.

The marvelous richness of human experience
would lose something of rewarding joy
if there were not limitations to overcome.
The hilltop hour would not be half
so wonderful if there were
no dark valleys to traverse.

Helen Keller

_____

_____

_____

_____

_____

_____

_____

_____

_____

_____

_____

_____

_____

_____

June 29

It was November in Beijing, and I was a student once again—joining 25 Chinese students in the study of the ancient healing art of Qigong. That was our only link as we didn't share a common culture, a common generation or even a common language.

With one student I felt an instant affinity. Our communication, though, took place without words.

Through our study of Qigong we were somewhat accustomed to exploring the realms beyond the intellect, but that drive to communicate with words held us in its clutches.

I went to my dorm and began teaching myself Chinese characters. If I could at least copy the ones I needed, I would be able to write my friend a note.

I set about to draw four characters that translated to "I happy you friend."

That evening I revealed the note, and she took it and put it in her pocket. Within two steps, she turned back toward me and offered me a piece of paper. It was folded origami-style into a swan and I made out four words: "I happy you friend."

Garri Garripoli

*R*onny had a speech impediment, wasn't reading or writing at grade-level, and had already been held back a year, making him eight years old in the first grade. His home life was a shambles.

I worked with all the students in the class on a one-on-one basis; by the end of the year, Ronny had made some progress, but hardly enough to bring him up to grade level. He was the only one who didn't know that, though.

A few weeks before the school year ended, I held an awards ceremony. I presented Ronny with his certificate for "Most Improved Reader" and a book—one of those Little Golden Books that cost 49 cents at the grocery store checkout. It was, I found out, the first book he had ever actually owned.

I asked Ronny to read to me, and he did—with more expression, clarity and ease than I'd ever thought possible. When he finished, he closed his book, stroked the cover and said with great satisfaction, "Good book."

At that moment I knew I would try to do what that author had done—care enough to write a story that changes a child's life.

Judith A. Chance

July 1

The humid, unrelenting heat of summer can be especially brutal on the pocketbook, so one rule in our house was: Don't waste the water.

It was almost midnight when I heard the kitchen faucet running for at least five minutes. I leaped out of bed, stuck my head around the corner and exploded, "Are you trying to put our last penny down the drain?"

Then I heard another noise coming from the kitchen—the unmistakable echo of my 10-year-old son's sobs. Then what I saw made me cry.

The kitchen that I had been too tired to clean before bed was spotless. Stunned that Christopher would take such initiative, and thoroughly disgusted with myself, I gently encircled him with my arms.

"Please forgive me. I should have taken the time to see what was happening before flying off the handle." Then, acting on impulse, I blurted out, "Go get your bathing suit on." In two minutes we were both outside with the sprinklers running full tilt.

And when the bill came, I paid it, knowing one simple truth: to err is human, but to be forgiven by your child is truly divine.

Susan H. Hubbs

Be careful not to jump to conclusions.

*A*dopting babies was a popular thing to do among show-business people in the 1930s. Gracie wanted to have children, and I wanted to make Gracie happy. We called a Catholic foundling home in Illinois, and months later they told us we could have a baby if we came to Evanston immediately.

Gracie picked the smallest baby with great big blue eyes. What surprised me most was how much space something so small could take up. Our kitchen became the operations center, and my former den became her nursery. As it turned out, Sandy was such a delight that we decided she should have a brother.

Gracie picked out our son Ronnie because he needed her most. He looked like a wrinkled little man and made Winston Churchill look handsome.

Ronnie had a tough first year. For a long time he couldn't gain weight, and his skin was so sensitive that we could only bathe him in oil and wrap him in cotton. But Ronnie was a smart kid, and once he figured out how to grow, he didn't stop until he was almost 6'2" tall and much better looking than Churchill.

Gracie had been right.

George Burns

July 3

I looked at my twin teenagers and wanted to cry. He wore baggy pants, orange hair and earrings. She wore a nose ring, a fake tattoo and three-inch nails. It was Passover, and we were on our way to the relatives . . . for dinner . . . to celebrate. What they had on—to them—was respectable, and so we went.

I was ready for the looks, but none came. I was ready for the whispers. None came. My kids sat around the table, participated in the service and sang the holiday songs.

I realized that it didn't matter what anyone else thought. Because I thought they were terrific. Sitting across the table, I knew that the hair, the baggy clothes and fake tattoos were just a statement of who they were for the moment. This would change with time. But their participation in the songs and ceremonies of our holidays and the closeness of our family would be with them always.

Later, I would tell them how great they were and how proud I was to be their mom.

Shari Cohen

July 4

*N*ot long after the New Year dawned, my husband, an F-16 pilot, and his comrades strapped into their jets and headed over the ocean. We wives banded together. We laughed together and cried together. We commiserated over all the household catastrophes that only happen when husbands are away. We didn't speak too much about our fears; those were understood. I thanked God for the strength of the wives.

When duty calls, the soldier will answer. In fact, he may seem eager to leave those he loves and fight the good fight. It is hard to be married to a hero.

A soldier is called to fight, and the spouse of a soldier is called to understand. Understanding makes you a hero, too.

Denise J. Hunnell

July 5

*I*nstinctively I knew, even at five, that this little bundle everyone cooed over would profoundly impact my life. My bedroom became "our" room. My things were constantly in the "share with your sister" pile.

As adults our rivalry became nothing more than an occasional annoyance, and we were the best of friends. Until the final competition . . . the one I couldn't overlook . . . involved my man! My sister moved in with us after her second divorce, and within six months, my husband, my house, my world belonged to her.

I went on with my life, raised my children, remarried and graduated from college at the age of 45. It wasn't until she called me to ask for help when she was getting a divorce . . . again, that I faced two painful truths:

1) My sister didn't break up my marriage, and
2) I wanted revenge for her betrayal.

I found that once I was able to honestly access the past—and forgive myself—I was no longer a victim. I understood that anger and hatred were choices—and I chose to let them go. I was free, and happiness at having my sister back in my life became my priority.

Diane Burke

Anger and hatred are a choice, and if you choose to let them go, you will be free.

You may have the loftiest goals, the highest ideals, the noblest dreams, but remember this, nothing works unless you do.

Nido Qubein

_____

_____

_____

_____

_____

_____

_____

_____

_____

_____

_____

_____

_____

_____

_____

_____

_____

July 7

There are days, like today, when I wonder why I am a teacher. Despite my best efforts, the world of pronouns remains a mystery to my fifth-graders. During lunch period, a child became sick and needed me to gather her assignments while she waited for her mother. Then an argument broke out at recess.

I can't seem to get out of my classroom ahead of the traffic, and as I sit, threaded behind a distant stoplight, I replay the day and revisit the tension. Then I remember why I'm still teaching. It's the children. They're more important than a lifetime filled with quiet evenings and more valuable than a pocket filled with money. The world of noise, pronouns, recess and homework is my world. My classroom, a child-filled world of discovery, kindness and caring is the real world. And I'm so lucky to be in it.

The traffic light clears, and I move into the shady streets of my neighborhood. It's time to call my friend and tell her I can't meet her tonight. She'll understand. She's a teacher.

Kris Hamm Ross

*N*o one tells us that the greatest moments of a lifetime are fleeting, unplanned and nearly always catch us off guard.

Not long ago, as I was reading a bedtime story to my seven-year-old daughter, I became aware of her focused gaze. I asked what she was thinking about.

"Mommy," she whispered, "I just can't stop looking at your pretty face."

I almost dissolved on the spot.

Not long after, I took my four-year-old son to an elegant department store, where the melodic notes of a classic love song drew us toward a tuxedoed musician playing the piano. As we sat and listened, Sam stood up next to me, took my face in his little hands and said, "Dance with me."

Although shoppers openly chuckled, grinned and pointed at us as we glided and whirled around the open atrium, I would not have traded a dance with such a charming young gentleman if I'd been offered the universe.

Jean Harper

The greatest moments of a lifetime are usually fleeting and unplanned.

July 9

My father had been diagnosed with dementia and lived in a nursing home. He became ill enough to be admitted to the hospital, so I stayed with him. He was confused and rarely spoke, but that didn't keep me from chatting away.

One day I ran out of things to say, so I decided to sing. Unfortunately, I inherited my daddy's musical ability. Neither of us could carry a tune in a bucket. I crooned, "I love you. You love me. We're a great big family."

Daddy opened his eyes, turned and looked at me. For the first time in days, he spoke. "I love you too, honey," he said, "but you don't have to sing about it."

Nancy B. Gibbs

It was no surprise to me when my mother was diagnosed with Alzheimer's. Over a period of years her optimistic eyes began to dim, and her mental agility began to disappear. Alzheimer's, a thief in slow motion, left a woman who could no longer remember her personal history. Her supposedly golden years were spent living in a house she never called home and enduring a sense of disorientation that she did not understand.

One morning, her arm threaded in mine, we strolled out of her group house for our walk around town. Suddenly, my boot wedged in a deep crevice in the walkway, and I was pitched forward. My mother reacted instantly, yanking me upright.

"Are you okay?" she asked with concern. My old mom, the mom I had always known, was smiling at me, not a trace of confusion evident.

"I love you so much," she said as she kissed me. "I don't want anything to happen to you."

Even though I see my mother often, I keep looking forward to the next time I might stumble across her endearing old self, feel her love wrap around me.

Sandra Rockman

Love is never forgotten.

July 11

It was one of those years when I found my inner voice whispering, "What else can go wrong?" Then September 11th happened. Life became a topsy-turvy struggle, and our marriage was faltering under the strain.

One afternoon, while out walking with my grand-daughter, I witnessed the most exceptional message of all from a flock of geese flying overhead in a perfect V formation. For some odd reason, one goose left the group and started to fly in an entirely different direction. The main flock completely changed its course and gradually picked up their wayward member. As I watched this simple display, I couldn't help but think of my family. Our lives too, it seemed, had gone astray for a while. But through courage, inner strength and pure love, our family would change its course and triumph.

Susan Siersma

*L*ast year Maya was in kindergarten. One day she came home from school, bubbling over with excitement. "Mama, guess what! There's a new girl in my class, and she doesn't speak any English, and I'm her new best friend. I decided today!"

I met Stephanie when it came time for the Halloween party. She was clearly scared and withdrawn. Never once smiling, she sat as the other kids played games.

The days flew by, and each day Maya came home from school babbling about how her day went, what Stephanie learned, etc. I was usually too busy to really listen to my daughter and never realized what I was missing until the day I went to teach her class sign language and saw Stephanie.

I couldn't believe the transformation. She still spoke very little English, but now she tried to participate. Most of her communication with Maya was pointing, helping, gesturing.

That night I told Maya how proud I was of her and asked her how she created this amazing friendship without a word of language. She looked up at me and said, "I smiled."

Farr-Fahncke

All it takes is a smile to reach out to someone.

July 13

For twelve years Jenna had lived courageously, fighting her chronic disease. I understood her feelings of defeat because I, too, was tired of watching my daughter tend to her catheter site, injecting herself with the proper medications and experiencing the unpredictable side effects.

What does a mother say to her child who is living a nightmare? What words could bring comfort when all hope is lost?

Not knowing the answers, I spoke from my heart.

"Jenna, I need to know that you really understand what I am about to say. Today you're tired and you've lost all hope. Today you can rest in my arms and let me hope for you. You can be assured that my hope is endless and so is my love."

Jenna interrupted me, smiling slightly. "If you can hope for me, I guess I can, too." She draped her arms around me. "Tell me again, Mom, that your hope is forever."

"It's forever, baby. My hope is forever."

Janet Lynn Mitchell

*The purpose of life, after all, is to live it,
to taste experience to the utmost, to reach out
eagerly and without fear for newer
and richer experiences.*

Eleanor Roosevelt

_____
_____
_____
_____
_____
_____
_____
_____
_____
_____
_____
_____
_____
_____
_____
_____

July 15

All too often, as parents and teachers, we convey to our children that nothing but top performance meets with our approval.

Donnie, my youngest third-grader, was a shy, nervous perfectionist. His fear of failure kept him from classroom games, he seldom answered questions, and written assignments reduced him to nail-biting frustration. Even Mary Anne, my student teacher, was baffled by this little boy who feared he might make a mistake.

Then one day, she took a canister filled with pencils from the desk we shared.

"See these pencils, Donnie? See how the erasers are worn? That's because Mrs. Lindstrom and I make mistakes, too. But we erase the mistakes and try again. That's what you must learn to do."

She stood up. "I'll leave one of these pencils so you'll remember that it's all right to make mistakes as long you erase them and try again."

Aletha Jane Lindstrom

Every child must learn
that it is all right to make mistakes.

*M*y friend Debbie's two daughters were in high school when she became pregnant with Tommy. As time went by, it seemed as though every day brought another reason to celebrate the gift of Tommy's life.

One day when Tommy was about five years old, he and Debbie were driving to the mall. As is the way with children, out of nowhere, Tommy asked, "Mom, how old were you when I was born?"

"Thirty-six, Tommy. Why?" Debbie asked.

"What a shame!" Tommy responded. "Just think of all those years we didn't know each other."

Alice Collins

July 17

While waiting for the light to change, I glimpsed a rather large, low-flying bird followed by her offspring taking its fledgling flight. Suddenly, the baby bird lost altitude, unable to stay aloft. The mother swooped down and lifted the baby on her back, then pulled away again. She moved a few feet to the side, and then a few feet below. Baby was doing fine. I drove slowly, observing my birds, thinking: *This is life!*

We release our young so many times, in so many ways: We help them take their first steps, wish them well as they go away to college and give them away in marriage. I thought of my daughter, now grown with a nine-month-old baby of her own, experiencing these same kinds of poignant moments that only a mother can understand.

As I opened the door from the garage, the phone began to ring. My daughter was calling from her home, fifteen hundred miles away, with news that her son had minutes earlier just taken his first steps.

Later I went for a walk on the beach. Birds soared overhead, and my grandson had started his journey through life. One step at a time.

Eileen Davis

My eldest son's final 24 hours as a full-time resident in our home went by too quickly for me. We drove home from the airport a different family. No longer a quartet, we were like a wobbly, three-legged table. As the first day without him ended, I visited my eldest's room and mourned for his boyhood. When nonstop crying brought me no comfort, I realized I needed a mechanism to help me accept the loss.

I remembered a widowed friend telling me she found comfort through observing the Jewish death ritual. The next morning, I began the week-long ritual of grieving, called sitting shiva. I watched old home movies, looked through photo albums, read his favorite books. While the traditional ritual of Jewish grieving is a year in length, I came to terms with my loss in several weeks. I began to think less about the boy and more about the man he had become.

In utilizing ritual to effect my own emotional recovery, I learned that the old ways may hold answers for parents of the New Age and that every parental crisis doesn't require reinventing the wheel.

Ellyn L. Geisel

When dealing with a crisis, sometimes the old ways are the best ways.

July 19

She slips into this world and into my arms. An indescribable gift, she opens her eyes, and I am transformed.

Lying on the bed, she sleeps between her daddy and me. We look for ways she looks like us and ways she is uniquely herself. We have nothing to say, but our hearts and minds are full of thoughts—of our hopes and dreams for her, of who she might be, of what gifts she brings with her and how she might touch the world.

As the days and years pass, we are awed at the transformation. She teaches us how to play again, to slow down and see the world again. To rediscover the things we used to see and know.

Time will fly; suddenly she will be grown, a young adult, ready to soar into the world and give what she came here for. Letting go will be wrenching, and yet we know that she is not ours to keep.

Jeanette Lisefski

*R*ecently a friend told me with great sadness about the falling-out she'd had with her sister shortly before her sister's death. One of my favorite cousins told me that her relationship with her beloved sister had become so fragile that she feared they would never repair the damage. This scenario isn't confined just to family. Friendships and other meaningful relationships are destroyed every day over mundane as well as profound issues.

If someone were to ask me what I would do if I "had it to do all over again," my answer would be this: I would love my friends and relations so well that no matter what, they would love me back in the same way. No reservations, no quid pro quos. No angst, no sibling rivalry, no holds barred. I say this because I lost my sister before I could reclaim her, and it was too late.

To everyone I would give the same advice. "No matter what your issues are, find your way back to what binds you. No matter what it takes, have it out until you get back in touch with the love, the loyalty, the special relationship you once had."

Elayne Clift

*The most important thing in life is to love
your friends and relations so well
that they will love you back, no matter what.*

July 21

*M*r. Degner," he began, "you probably don't remember meeting me and my family. We were going to Miami, and the flight was overbooked. You asked for volunteers to give up their seats for free tickets and a later flight. We gave you our tickets, but later you came back and said you wouldn't need our tickets after all, and you had upgraded us to first class."

The story still didn't ring a bell. He continued: "The flight to Miami was wonderful, but there is something else. Just after we got home from our vacation, Nathan was out riding his bike . . . The driver never saw him. That trip was the last week the four of us were together. We'll always remember that flight. We were so happy, and Nathan had so much fun. I just wanted to say how much we appreciate the gift you gave us."

Months later Nathan's father visited me at the airport and gave me a picture of his son. I keep it as a constant reminder that the smallest gesture can touch others in an unexpected and extraordinary way.

Jeff Degner

There are no small gestures.

*D*aydreams were a way of life for me. They provided an escape from the mundane life I led. I spent many waking hours enjoying the illusion of wealth, fame and leisure—and had even begun to plot and scheme to manipulate myself out of the relationships that held me back from a life of sophistication, adventure and pleasure.

One sunny afternoon, I was driving down a country highway when a big semitruck unexpectedly veered to the right. A red Yugo flew upward over the truck, passed by the side of my station wagon and nosedived into the highway with a dull clunk, rear wheels spinning in the sky.

I rushed to the car and felt for a pulse. At that moment the man lifted his head, took a deep breath, looked me straight in the eye and managed to murmur, "Tell them I love . . . ," and then he died.

I held his hand until the ambulance arrived. As I drove away, a sense of inner joy and sincere appreciation for life entered my heart. An unknown man's final thoughts were not of riches or fame, but of the people he loved, and his words became a candle in the dark just for me.

Lynne Zielinski

July 23

> *If the winds of fortune are temporarily*
> *blowing against you, remember that*
> *you can harness them and make them*
> *carry you toward your definite purpose,*
> *through the use of your imagination.*
>
> *Napoleon Hill*

_____

_____

_____

_____

_____

_____

_____

_____

_____

_____

_____

_____

_____

_____

July 24

Our daughter Ariana moved from baby to toddler with her share of the usual bumps and scraped knees. On these occasions, I'd hold out my arms and say, "Come see me." She'd crawl into my lap and I'd say, "Are you my girl? My sweetie, beetie Ariana girl?" She'd nod her head and I'd end with, "And I love you forever, for always, and no matter what!"

A few weeks ago I reached my breaking point one afternoon and went into my room for a good cry.

Ariana soon came to my side and said, "Come see me." She curled up beside me and said, "Are you my mommy? My sweetie, beetie mommy?" I nodded my head and smiled. "And I love you forever, for always, and no matter what!" A giggle, a big hug, and I was off and ready for my next challenge.

Jeanette Lisefski

July 25

*A*s we walked around the grounds, I noticed the old orphanage had really lost its luster. My wife and I were coming to meet her friend who hoped I'd be a surrogate parent to one of the boys there.

The 14-year-old extended his hand in greeting. His limp handshake felt like a rubber glove full of pudding. "Thank you for coming to visit my home."

I excused myself and walked into the bathroom. For about a minute, I looked at every wrinkle and sag on my face, yet it was still the face of that same little boy I was when I lived in my orphanage, almost 45 years ago.

I placed my right hand into my left and shook it. It was a bit firmer than that of young Bill's, but it still lacked the feeling of someone who felt they were worth loving.

Biting my lip, I stared deep into my own eyes and said to myself, "Let's go save that boy."

Let there be no doubt that when we save a child, in the process we may also save ourselves.

Roger Dean Kiser, Sr.

embe and I found each other in a hot, dry field in the south of Turkey. I was walking, and she was watching her goats graze. She approached, talking Turkish and seemed irritated that I did not respond. Taking my hand, Pembe escorted me across the field to a small gray shack.

We entered her house through a crowded kitchen and living room. Pembe pushed down on my shoulders, telling me to sit. Then she resumed shouting her Turkish phrases at me. I matched her energy, repeating her words back.

Two hours later, we walked together, arm in arm, out of her house and over to the fence that separated her land from the villa where my group was staying. There, Pembe said good-bye—"guli guli"—in a quiet voice and waved.

Now when I hear the news of deaths and disaster caused by an earthquake, Turkey is no longer a faraway, somewhat obscure place on a map. It is a country of apricots, goat cheese, golden fields of grass, dancing children and wise women wearing the wide, patched pants of everyday life.

Heidi Ehrenreich

July 27

Over the years, we have traveled and lived in many different places, and many people have touched our lives in ways I will never forget.

While my husband was on temporary duty in Africa, I took my two girls home to give them some time with their grandparents. After an hour on the road, I pulled off the interstate and stopped at a gas station. A while later, I stopped again, reached for my wallet . . . and it was gone. I knew there was little to no possibility of my wallet being found, much less returned, as I had no current address or phone numbers in it.

But the next day a girl called from Blockbuster Video.

"Someone has found your wallet and is waiting here at our store."

It seems a couple and the woman's mother were on a day trip, and the mother, who was a smoker, set herself on fire. "I pulled over to brush off the ashes, and as I was walking behind the car I saw your wallet," she said.

This family went out of their way to find the Blockbuster Video with the hope of the store being able to find me.

Lisa Cobb

**People will go out of their way
and make every effort to help others.**

When I fell and hurt myself, my mother would take my hand in hers and say, "When it hurts, squeeze my hand, and I'll tell you that I love you." Sometimes I'd pretend I'd been hurt just to have that ritual with her. As I grew up, the ritual changed, but she always found a way to ease the pain and increase the joy I felt.

One morning, when I was in my late thirties, my father phoned me at work. "Mary, something's wrong with your mother."

When I arrived at their house, Mom was lying on their bed, her eyes closed and her hands resting on her stomach. "Mom, I'm here."

"Mary, I hurt so much. Am I going to die?"

I paused for a moment, waiting for the words to come. I picked up her hand and heard myself say, "Mom, when it hurts, squeeze my hand, and I'll tell you that I love you."

She squeezed my hand.

"Mom, I love you."

Many hand squeezes and "I love you's" passed between my mother and me during the next two years, until she passed away from ovarian cancer.

Mary Marcdante

July 29

$\mathcal{M}$ary Jane, my best friend and speaking partner for over 25 years, had been fighting colon cancer for seven years. As I walked past the front desk at the hospice center, I noticed a lemon meringue pie on the counter and brought it to Mary Jane.

I gave her just enough for her to taste the essence of lemon before her ravaged body rejected it. "Gee, thanks. That was great."

"How could you say that was great?"

"I've been thinking," she said. "It's all the moments leading up to and directly after an event—the minutes and hours that define how we respond to it. We've got to focus on the space between events."

She continued, "It's the excitement that comes from watching your team before they actually score. The memory of home sparked by the smell of lemons as you lift a forkful of pie to your lips." She squeezed my hand. "The space between events is where most of life is lived ... and it is in this space, my friend, that you and all caregivers must also focus."

Pamela J. Gordon

Focus on the space between events because that is where most of life is lived.

*B*rendan cried his first day of school. It wasn't that he didn't like school. Brendan just didn't like being apart from me.

We'd had some good times in his preschool years, but now in first grade, Brendan was faced with five hours of wondering what I was doing with my day. He told me once that he watched me until he couldn't see me any more, so when I dropped him off at school, I always walked fast and never looked back.

But one day—I don't know why—I glanced back. The playground buzzed all around him, and there he was, so completely loving, watching me go.

My mind leaped ahead 15 years to him packing boxes and saying, "Dry up, Mom. It's not like I'm leaving the country."

I looked at my Brendan and I thought, *Okay, you're six for me forever. Just try to grow up, I dare you.* With a smile I had to really dig for, I blew him a kiss, turned and walked away.

Diane Tullson

July 31

> *Keep away from people who try*
> *to belittle your ambitions.*
> *Small people always do that, but*
> *the really great make you feel*
> *that you, too, can become great.*
>
> *Mark Twain*

_____

_____

_____

_____

_____

_____

_____

_____

_____

_____

_____

_____

_____

*H*er hair has been set in steel curlers, permed, styled in pageboys, the poodle look and the beehive hairdo.

She has earned her nursing degree through measles, chicken pox, mumps, pneumonia, fevers, stitches, fractured arms and broken hearts.

She has journeyed through life with its tears and laughter. Her heart has known the ecstasy of a man's love, the joy of children, the heartbreak of their mistakes, the warmth of life's friendships, the celebration of weddings, the magnificent blessings of grandchildren and great-grandchildren.

When a mother blows out 75 candles, blessed are they who surround her with their love.

Alice Collins, submitted by Geraldine Doyle

August 2

I was an only child, hungry for siblings. My first sister was my imaginary playmate, Punky. We were inseparable until the first time the yellow school bus stopped for me. Punky was left behind.

At school I fell off the monkey bars, and Susie brushed me off and led me to the nurse's office for repairs. In high school, my circle of sisterhood widened. Lipstick and secret information about the heartthrob of the day were freely shared. We celebrated love and cried together when love ended.

My collegiate sisters came from different places and offered me glimpses of other lives. Until graduation, when we moved back to our own worlds.

I have been blessed with adult sisters who have mentored and shared my travails as wife, mother and teacher. We listened to tales about recalcitrant bosses and professional successes. When aging parents orphaned us, tears and hugs gave comfort like no words could.

At every turn I have found my sisters. They have flowed through my life, renewing and enriching me with their presence. And I can't wait to meet the next one.

Lee Schafer Atonna

$\mathcal{I}$t was the year of the Olympics, and I had accepted a fifth-grade teaching position in Atlanta. This was a diverse group of students who were tolerant of the differences of others. We began to study the different countries that were preparing for the games and discussed how every person's role on a team was important.

By spring, I began a project called Goals and Dreams, where each class would set a goal and all the students would participate to make it happen.

They decided to train for a 3.1-mile race the school sponsored to raise money for cancer research. Everyone was excited except Luke, the largest boy in the class. He understood that winning didn't matter, but coming in last would be humiliating.

The day of the race I stood with the parents, greeting the students as they crossed the finish line. Soon, there was no sign of Luke or of my students and their parents. Then I heard a commotion around the final bend before the finish line.

Suddenly, I saw Luke, surrounded by all 26 fifth-graders, cheering him on. Together they crossed the finish line, screaming, with Luke as their hero.

Jodi O'Meara

August 4

My mother and I shared a house with my grandmother and my aunt and uncle. That Depression Christmas, jobs were scarce and money tight. I understood why my pile of presents under the tree was so small, but I still felt a guilty twinge of disappointment. I knew there would be a new book for me, but none of the hoped-for indulgences of Christmas. But there was one fairly big box from my grandmother, and I opened it last.

Socks! Nothing but socks. My grandmother was smiling a sparkling, happy, "This is important woman-to-woman stuff, so pay attention!" smile.

I looked down at the box, but now I could see there was another pair under the pair I had picked up. Two layers of socks. Three layers of socks!

"Merry Christmas, Joan," my grandmother said. "Every day now you'll have an abundance of choices to make. You're rich, my dear."

That was a Christmas I'll never forget. My grandmother's gift showed me how wonderful and important little things can be and how enormously wealthy love makes us all.

Joan Cinelli

Little things can be wonderful and important, and love makes everyone wealthy.

*M*y 90-year-old mom, Bert, is in the late stages of Alzheimer's disease. She is in a nursing home. Once a fun, witty woman, now she rarely has lucid moments, and we communicate primarily through touch.

One day, an aide in the nursing home went to check on my mother. She was shocked to find Mom on the floor, with no apparent injury, still asleep and snoring. The aide called to the nurse who immediately headed to the room, saying, "Bert doesn't move. She doesn't roll. This can't be."

The aide wondered out loud, "Maybe we should pull up the bed rails."

From my mother came, "Don't you think it's a little late for that now?"

Esther Copeland

August 6

*M*artha Lindsay had waited 13 months for hope that her husband, William, had survived the sinking of the *H.M.S. Exeter* in 1942. Then she received word from the Red Cross that a William Lindsay was a prisoner of war.

She was instructed to write one message a month, no more than 25 words on a plain white postcard, and forward them to Geneva. Two and a half years passed before the mailman delivered a small scrap of paper. She turned it over and recognized William's handwriting: "Martha, I've been released. I'm coming home."

In October 1945, William Lindsay returned to his family. Martha learned, sadly, that not one of her letters had found its way to the camp.

Shortly after William's arrival home, a young sailor appeared at the door. "My name is William Lindsay. I was a prisoner of war." Very slowly he reached into his pocket and handed her 30 tiny white postcards tied in a ribbon.

"I received one every month. They were the glimmer of hope that helped me survive. From the bottom of my heart, thank you."

Shelley McEwan

When my nine-year-old son saw his baby-sitter kissing her boyfriend, he wanted to know, "What's so great about all this kissing and love stuff?"

I decided to tell my son that first kisses and first loves have to be experienced to be understood. I explained that the symptoms were like coming down with the flu.

He seemed satisfied with that answer, and I forgot about our heart-to-heart until yesterday when my now 14-year-old came home with a slightly glazed look in his eye and a sappy grin on his face. I asked him if he was feeling okay. As he breezed past me on his way to the fridge, he said, "I hate to admit it, Mom, but you were right. It does feel like the flu. But don't worry, it's probably only a twenty-four-hour bug, and I'll be fine by tomorrow." I asked him how he could be so sure. "Oh, that's easy," he said. "She's not enough like you to make me really sick."

Eileen Goltz

August 8

A woman is like a tea bag.
You never know how strong
she is until she gets into hot water.

Eleanor Roosevelt

_____

_____

_____

_____

_____

_____

_____

_____

_____

_____

_____

_____

_____

_____

*M*y son Ryan had set his heart on exploring Europe after high school. We had visited many countries together, and he was familiar with what to expect, but this time he wanted to do it alone. I had given him a long-distance calling card, but I still worried nonstop.

The days and weeks slipped by, and my son's calls came with increasing frequency. Soon, he was calling every second day, and there was a curious tone in his voice that made me wonder.

Needless to say, I was happy and not entirely surprised when out of the blue he told me that he had decided to come home.

At the airport, Ryan was the first to speak. "Mom," he said, "I have learned so much about myself and what's important. I know that no matter where you go in the world and what you see, you need someone to share it with in order to make it special."

And I felt pride in the fact that I had said good-bye to a child, but a mature young man had come home, and he was my son.

Penny Fedorcaenko

Sharing an experience with someone can make it special.

August 10

Almost five years ago at her eightieth-birthday celebration, my mother, feeling fine and looking wonderful, closed her eyes and died in my living room.

To me she had been larger than life. She was fiery and funny. She was brave and honest, but most of all, she was compassionate.

Time has passed and healed us all. Slowly I recalled things she said to me in the months before she died. One night she said, "You are so kind, Terry, so compassionate, and you bring such light into people's lives. You have that gift: a talent for liveliness...." I stopped her there.

"Mom! That's not me you're describing; it's you." But she would have none of that.

Every day of my life since then, I have worn her large-faced watch. Always, I tell her stories. "You know, you sound a lot like your mother," people tell me more and more lately.

And I sense that the woman who mothered me is someplace not far off. Inside, or all around. In a sudden familiar twinkle in the eyes of one of my children. Even in my very mirror.

Terry Marotta

As we get older, we grow more and more like our mothers.

$\mathcal{I}$ was sent to stay with my grandmother when I was 16 years old. I was a very troubled young woman, ready to drop out of school. I thought my grandmother would be easier to ignore than my parents.

I expected nothing from my grandmother but to be left alone. She, however, did not give up so easily. So, I shouldn't have been surprised when she insisted I learn to make bread. I was a failure at kneading, but she wouldn't let me leave the kitchen until the bread was set out to rise. It was then that I first began to talk to her.

One day I announced, "I was named editor of the high-school newspaper!"

She looked into my eyes and said, "I like you so much, and I am very proud of you!"

Those words did more for me than a thousand "I love you's." I knew her love was unconditional, but her friendship and pride were things to earn. To receive them both from this incredible woman made me begin to wonder whether there was something likable and worthy within myself. On that day, I decided to live as she did—with energy and intensity.

Lynnette Curtis

August 12

*W*hen it comes to other people's fortunes, I think I have been downright magnanimous. But there's only so much we hard-working non-millionaires can take.

Recently, I came into an unexpected inheritance. Not enough to buy a Tuscan villa, but enough to make me think that perhaps I should hop aboard America's Investment Express.

I consulted a highly regarded financial planner who recommended certain mutual funds that he'd be willing to put his own money into if his portfolio weren't so darn diversified.

However, while NASDAQ was setting new records, my little nest egg was, apparently, helping to support ventures like fisheries in the Ganges and accordion start-ups in Warsaw.

After the third consecutive quarter of double-digit losses, I begin to see things more clearly. With a cool million or two available at the ATM, would that morning cup of French roast taste any richer? Would the sight of a good friend's face be more welcome? Would the colors of a sunset be more beautiful with a bigger bank balance? No, I decide. Definitely not. Riches have little to do with real contentment.

And yes, Regis, that is my final answer.

Sue Diaz

Riches have little to do with real contentment.

August 13

*I*t had been a long, tiring day caring for my husband, and when he spit the pill out, I was upset and said in an unkind voice, "Why did you do that?"

"But that's what you told me to do, isn't it?" he said softly.

I began to cry. The doctor had told me that he might begin processing language in reverse. How could I have been so cross with him, when he had done what he understood me to say?

When he saw me crying, he reached out to me. "Don't cry. Come here." Moving over by his wheelchair, I put my head on his knee, and he patted my shoulder.

Although he didn't understand my asking him to swallow the pill, he did understand my distress and pain, and his love caused him to reach out to comfort me.

These gestures spoke to me as eloquently as if he had spoken out loud, proving where there is love, there will never be an insurmountable language barrier.

Dorothy Snyder

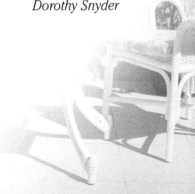

August 14

My principal's office was right next door to the health clinic, so I often dropped in to lend a hand and help out with the hugs.

One day, I ran across an unfamiliar lump under my arm. I pondered whether or not to tell the students about my cancer. Even though I decided to tell them myself, it wasn't easy to get out the words. As the children solemnly filed out of the gym, one little girl said earnestly, "Don't be afraid, Dr. Perry. I know you'll be back because now it's our turn to take care of you."

They sent me off to my first chemotherapy session with a hilarious book of nausea remedies that they had written. A video of every class singing get-well songs accompanied me to the next appointment. By the third, the nurses were waiting to see what I would bring next.

When I went into isolation for a bone-marrow transplant, the letters and pictures kept coming. What healing comfort I found in being surrounded by these tokens of their caring.

As my little buddy said when I was well enough to return to work: "See, I told you we'd take care of you!"

Suzanne M. Perry

August 15

Do not follow where the path may lead.
Go, instead, where there is no path
and leave a trail.

Ralph Waldo Emerson

_____

_____

_____

_____

_____

_____

_____

_____

_____

_____

_____

_____

_____

_____

_____

August 16

As a single mother I tended to dwell on my shortcomings—how many evenings I had to spend poring over textbooks to earn my college degree; the number of things I couldn't stretch my salary to buy.

One year Denny, my "baby," was home from college. I padded to the kitchen to start breakfast and was greeted by a vase containing a dozen red roses and a note:

> *She took a day off from her busy schedule to take the boy to see his hero in the flesh at the stadium. It took three-and-a-half hours just to get there. On their arrival she took her hard-earned money to buy an overpriced T-shirt portraying his hero making a diving catch. After the game he had to get his hero's autograph, so she stayed with the little boy until one o'clock in the morning in spite of her alarm clock would ring early. It took me long enough to realize it, but I finally know who the real hero is.*
>
> *Denny McCormick and Lisa McCormick*

After depositing my son's pajamas in his drawer one too many days in a row, I turned to him and said, "You need to put your own pajamas away. I'm not your slave!"

"What's a slave?" he asked.

"A slave," I explained, "is someone who has to work but doesn't get paid for it."

The rest of the morning I worked hard: the only thing I took pleasure in that morning was my shower. And that was interrupted halfway through by both kids pounding on the bathroom door.

After putting my daughter down for her afternoon nap and quietly slipping out of her room, I turned around. There in the hall was my son, holding a handful of coins. "Here," he said, giving them to me. "Now you're not a slave."

I thought about it for a minute and decided he was right. For a total of 13 cents, he bought my freedom.

Christie A. Hansen

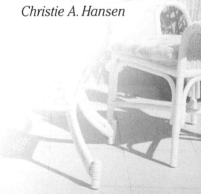

August 18

I am an ocean person, though I have lived most of my life away from the sea I love so much. As a single mother of four, I felt like I was marking time in the wrong place.

On my forty-second birthday, my sister gave me a trip to see the gray whale migration outside of Tofino on the wild West Coast I longed for.

It was as perfect an experience as it could be, and when it was over I went back to my hope, to my hated job, and to a persistent depression. I did, however, write a letter to the woman who had taken me to see the whales, telling her how lucky she was to be living her dream.

Just when I had won a promotion and was earning enough money to not have to worry about food and bills, a letter came from Tofino.

I learned that there is an inner voice that will guide us each and every step of the way when we slow down and choose to listen. It took enormous courage, but I followed my heart and made my dreams come true.

Sherry Baker

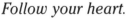

Follow your heart.

hree months before my first child was born, I began gathering baby things. I already had some clothes of mine, some of my dad's that my grandmother had saved, and some that my mother and grandmother had crocheted years before.

I'm not very good at crafts, but it was important to me to handmake the pillows and quilts and skirts for a bassinet. Then I went shopping.

She arrived on her due date in the tradition of the great Caesar. When she was placed in my arms, I looked down at her face and said, "Hi."

When it was time to bring her home, we dressed her in Dad's delicate baby dress and small, pretty cap and a pair of the crocheted booties.

The first friends we talked to asked what she looked like and I blurted out, "She looks like us!" Before that moment, I hadn't even thought about it. But 10 months later, someone else thought she did, too: the judge who approved our adoption.

Colleen Judy Farris

August 20

On Kara's twenty-sixth birthday we ran the Race for the Cure, an annual fundraiser for breast cancer. Kara and I had practiced staying together by holding a bungee chord between us because crowds frighten my Seeing Eye dog.

"On your mark! Get set! Go!" yells the starter. Finally, slowly, we begin to move. Soon, we are having fun. We're proud of ourselves, not only because we pass the walkers, but we're now up with the runners. I hear my friend Eve cheering us on from the sidelines.

We cross the finish line and slow to a walk. We settle on the grass as survivors tell their stories. It is one of the most moving and touching experiences we will ever share, not just as mother and daughter, but as two women.

The bungee chord lies between us in the grass, but its meaning will continue to give me strength and courage. Connection is what it's all about, one child to her mother, one woman to another.

Mary Hiland

"Caregiver" is a word that was foreign to me when I was young. Growing up and being independent was my goal. Then, in college, I met you. We made our vows in a lovely garden wedding, and when our first child was born, we loved being parents.

When we were young, naive newlyweds, hearing the words "demyelinating disease" for the first time, and understanding I probably had multiple sclerosis, left me stunned. My first reaction was to move back home with my mom, send you back home to yours and forget we were ever married. Solidly grounded in your commitment to our marriage, you said we would forge ahead and make it.

My daily needs are now your daily activities, and you do these things without complaint, without hesitation and with consistent dedication. Now that I've had MS for 21 years, my admiration for you has grown more than words can express.

Holly Baker

August 22

When Marissa was six months old, it seemed she was always looking up. I learned the magic of leaves dancing on trees and the awesome size of the tail of a jet. At eight months she was forever looking down.

Then she turned 11 months and began saying "Wow!" She spoke this marvelous word for anything new and wonderful to her. She whispered "Oh, wow!" for things that really impressed her. Then there was the ultimate in "Wow," a mouthing of the word with no sound.

She has taught me many ways to say "I love you." One day she pointed to a beautiful model on the cover of a magazine and said, "Is that you, Mom?" Most recently my now three-year-old walked into the kitchen while I was cleaning up and offered to help. Shortly after this she put her hand on my arm and said, "Mom, if you were a kid, we'd be friends."

At moments like this, all I can say is, "Oh, wow!"

Janet S. Meyer

*S*arah and I spent the summer before she went off to college sniping at each other. My friend, Pat, remembered the weeks before her daughter left home.

"We fought all summer long. I think it was our way of getting used to the idea of living apart. When you're arguing all the time, you don't feel so bad about her leaving."

On moving day, we helped her unpack and store her belongings in the dorm room. After lunch, we said good-bye, hugged at the curb, and then Chuck and I drove away.

Two days later I walked by her bedroom. Suddenly, it dawned on me: She's gone, and nothing would ever be the same. I wanted to call her, but Chuck said we should give her a week to settle in.

After dinner the phone rang. "Hi, Mom," Sarah said. "Could you send me a few things?"

She wanted her teddy bear, a photo of her father and me—and one of her younger brother. She loved being at school, but she missed us, too. And then she started telling me about her day, her classes, her teachers, her friends, the boys she liked, the boys who liked her. . . .

Beth Copeland Vargo

August 24

One must learn the thing, for though
you think you know it,
you have no certainty until you try.

Aristotle

_____
_____
_____
_____
_____
_____
_____
_____
_____
_____
_____
_____
_____
_____

*M*y friend's brother, Cliff, is a very serious, dignified man, so his actions at an airport's check-in counter were totally unexpected.

He and his wife were placing their baggage on the conveyor when her purse accidentally fell onto the moving belt. She scrambled after it but it eluded her, so she climbed onto the belt to try to reach it.

Just as she was about to disappear through the doorway with the baggage, Cliff began to wave frantically, "No, no dear!" he shouted. "It's okay! This time we bought tickets."

Jim Feldman

> *Doing the unexpected creates*
> *humor out of a serious situation.*

August 26

My husband was almost halfway through his third tour in Vietnam, and my near future would include the delivery of our fourth baby. I missed my husband, I was tired, and the weight of my bulging belly was pulling on my back. The 40 extra pounds on my normally thin body made me feel fat and ugly. I just couldn't seem to shake the blues.

My thoughts were interrupted by someone at the front door. There was a florist with a big box of flowers in his arms.

I thought the delivery was an error, but my name was on the box. I opened the card and smiled broadly. Since that morning, any time I feel sad, I draw on the joy I felt as I stood in the living room holding those flowers. There were only two words, but they were the ones I most needed: "Hello, beautiful!"

Jane Garvey

*The right words can make
all the difference in the world.*

*Y*ears ago when I first heard the term "empty nest," it sounded like a pleasant position to be in. However, when I reached that sought-after goal, it was rather a disappointment. Just when the children became pleasant company, they moved out.

When I finally crept out of my depression, I noticed my dear husband, Jack, looking almost the same as when I had fallen wildly in love with him. Except for showing a little wear and tear, the years had been good to him. I fondly looked at the gray hairs at his temple, knowing exactly where they had come from.

I realized my nest was not empty after all. It held the one special person I had chosen to share my life with. As I looked at him I wondered if maybe we could rekindle the sparks we had originally ignited. And then, as if to answer my unspoken question, he looked up at me and winked.

June Cerza Kolf

August 28

worried about my elderly neighbor's loneliness and her diet. Heart failure had robbed Gwen of her husband, and now macular degeneration was stealing her eyesight, and osteoporosis was plundering her body.

My life was on a fast track, so I turned to Koy, our three-year-old, for help.

With me watching from our front door and Gwen waiting at hers, Koy cautiously crossed the street, carrying the plate of fragrant food. And so began their long relationship.

Their regular visits continued through the years, sometimes at her invitation and other times at his instigation. As his age, sensitivity and caregiving expertise grew, Koy ran her errands, did light chores and drove her to doctor's appointments.

Finally, as we stood arm-in-arm waving Koy off to college, Gwen turned to me. "You know, when he was little he rarely came empty-handed. But when you didn't send something, he must have raided the pantry." She winked. "Over he would come, his pockets filled with raisins, pretzels, popcorn or even Cheerios."

"What did you do?" I laughed in motherly embarrassment.

"Well, the two of us sat down and ate them, pocket lint and all."

Carol McAdoo Rehme

Two years after an ectopic pregnancy and a bleak diagnosis for ever conceiving, my husband and I decided to adopt a baby. We retained an adoption attorney and placed ads in newspapers throughout the state.

Julia was four months pregnant, unwed, young and poor. Over the next few months we helped Julia with expenses, and I had nightly conversations with her about her health and welfare, which is why it was so incredibly devastating when Julia decided to keep her baby.

I continued to place ads. Then my lawyer called. Aurea was from the Philippines. She needed to go home, but being unwed, there was no way she could take her baby boy with her. It was agreed that Aurea would place her baby with us.

By the end of the next week, she placed him in my arms and hugged me close, whispering in my ear, "Please take care of my baby."

We never changed our son's first name. It was the best gift we could give him and Aurea. He is now 12 years old, and Aurea's act of kindness lives on daily in our hearts and souls.

Phyllis DeMarco

Sometimes our light goes out but is blown into flame by another human being. Each of us owes deepest thanks to those who have rekindled this light.

Albert Schweitzer

_____

_____

_____

_____

_____

_____

_____

_____

_____

_____

_____

_____

_____

_____

_____

*H*enning around, we called it. Getting together with a sister or two and doing girl stuff. This weekend six hens are having a reunion—sans husbands and children—at a cottage on a lake. We canoe, swim, work on our tans. Two us bike the county trails and play tennis; three shop. Miss Solitude claims the hammock for hours of uninterrupted quiet.

Later, over plates of linguine and crusty bread, we share the day, and under the onyx sky, the talk turns to the usual: old boyfriends, the best songs to slow-dance to, the most romantic thing our partners ever did. A sleepy hush falls over us like fleece.

"Bedtime," sing-songs one of the moms. No one begs for five more minutes.

Our last morning, we sweep the floors, straighten the beds and say good-bye to the lake, until next time.

Henning around. Just some chicks leaving the nest for a while, in search of nothing special. And finding it. Special.

Chris Miota

***When women get together
to do nothing special, they
sometimes find something very special.***

September 1

"I don't want a new baby."

This was my oldest son Brian's response when I told him his father and I were expecting a third child. We'd survived the first round of sibling rivalry when his brother, Damian, was born. But now three-year-old Brian had made his stand about this new baby.

Puzzled, I asked him, "Why don't you want a new baby?"

With wide and teary eyes, he looked straight at me and said, "Because I want to keep Damian."

Rosemary Laurey

*O*ne morning, as Angelito was getting ready for a run, his wife Evangeline noticed a lump on his upper thigh. After a two-year battle, Angelito lost his life. Evangeline was left alone with their three children. She managed to care for their needs, but each night she would go to bed alone and cry herself to sleep.

Her dear friend recognized this particular agony. One day, precisely at 5:00 P.M., which was the time when Angelito used to walk through the door, she insisted that Evangeline join her for a walk. After that, her friend came every day. During these walks, Evangeline would cry and cry. Her friend just quietly walked beside her, hour after hour, day after day.

They walked in rainstorms. They walked in the summer heat. Winter, spring, summer and fall, these two friends walked the road of grief together. This friend walked beside Evangeline for three years! Not a day was Evangeline left alone during "the big hour"; not until her friend sensed that she was strong enough to walk alone.

Evangeline Dionisio as told to Shelly Mecum

September 3

On September 3, 1959, I gave birth to a little boy, and though I saw him once, lying in the nursery, I was not allowed to hold him. Shortly after the birth I signed the adoption papers, and, as my doctor had suggested, I continued on with my life.

The years passed and turned into decades, and the memory of my only child lingered just beneath my conscious mind.

In 1993, I received the phone call I had fantasized about for years. "Elizabeth," Susie said, "I adopted your beautiful baby boy thirty-three years ago, and I am just calling to tell you what a wonderful son you have. Bill is married to a terrific girl, and you have two absolutely beautiful little granddaughters."

On the flight to Los Angeles, I wrote 33 birthday cards to my son with a short description of what I had done for each year of his life. Bill needs to learn about me, too.

When he saw me, Bill stepped from behind his wife and walked toward me with arms open wide. Into this circle of love I stepped, feeling just like every other mother in the world holding her baby for the first time.

Elizabeth Thring

*E*verything seemed to be against Kelly. But she had one person on her side: her first-grade teacher, Mrs. Dina. Nothing could take away the joy she felt from being with her teacher, and bit by bit, the hardness inside Kelly began to soften. Until one day her mother came to take her out of the school forever.

The following years were not kind to the young girl. By middle school, her mother had abandoned her, and she was placed in foster care. Somewhere she found the fortitude to continue on with her education to become an art teacher.

Assigned to a familiar place for student teaching, she heard a familiar kind voice, and there was Mrs. Dina.

Acting on instinct, she walked up to the woman and asked if she remembered her.

"Why, Kelly! How wonderful to see you again!"

"I am so glad I finally have the chance to thank you."

"Thank me? Whatever for? I only had you for a few months."

"But those were the few months that rescued the rest of my life."

Robin Lee Shope

September 5

A few weeks before Anny was to leave for college, I took the four girls to the beach. The sun was high and hot as we unloaded our gear and slathered on sunscreen. The three older girls went down to the water's edge to look for shells and get their toes wet. Elli settled down next to me with a shovel and pail, but after a few minutes, she asked if she could go down to the water with her sisters.

To my surprise, the older girls agreed to watch Elli and let her gather some shells. I watched them walk down the beach, the two older ones in front, Kayla next, Elli trailing behind. Every so often, one of them would call to the others, bend down, pick up some found treasure and put it in Elli's pail. But I noticed that Elli was not looking for shells. She was watching her sisters and seemed to be hopping from side to side, following directly behind them. Sometimes the older three walked side by side, but Elli always stayed behind.

It took me a few minutes, but then I realized what she was doing. Elli was walking in her sisters' footprints.

Marsha Arons

September 6

What was supposed to be an eight-day hospital stay and single surgery had turned into four surgeries, three months in the hospital, and then a nursing home because of aggressive infections and related complications. My husband, Terry, had performed the 6:00 A.M. and midnight wet-to-dry dressings on my abdomen and chest for several months.

One night we had an argument. By bedtime, we had to make up, and he still had the complicated dressing changes to complete.

Terry helped me roll onto my side. I sensed tension in the air. I looked up at him and said, "This isn't fair. I feel too vulnerable here with nothing on while you take care of my wounds when you're still mad at me."

He walked away, returned a few minutes later and stood in front of me. He was stark naked.

"Terry, what are you doing?" I shrieked with laughter.

"Just leveling the playing field," he smirked—then tenderly changed my dressing.

Linda S. Lee

Love and caring can take strange forms.

*J*oyfully, our adoption process was nearing the finale! When my newborn son was placed into my arms, the one nagging fear that had been tugging at my heart was overshadowed by the sheer joy of holding him. But the day the paperwork became final, I wondered where and when and how he would ask me the inevitable question: Are you my real mother?

I read and reread all the books and pamphlets explaining the "right" answers to be given at all the "appropriate" age levels. One night, as I was preparing dinner, my three-year-old came and stood beside me.

"Mommy," he blinked, trying to hold back the tears, "Sarah says you aren't my real mommy. She was wrong, right, Mommy?"

"Touch my hand," I slowly said. "Do I feel real to you?" I asked.

"You do!" he said as a smile broke across his face.

"Then I am your real mother, and my love for you is real."

It had happened. The question had been asked, and I had answered. I knew, in another time and place, there would be other, harder questions. But for now . . . I had done well.

Mary Chavoustie

The truth is the best answer.

*A*s teenagers, our children didn't always come right out and tell us where we, their parents, were going wrong. Instead, they had tricky little ways of reminding us that they were capable of outgrowing childhood.

When my husband and I had made the decision to go out of town for the weekend, I naturally left a long list of reminders. When we returned home, the kids were at school, but they had left a note that read:

Dear Mom,

Unpack your suitcase.

Have supper ready for us at six.

Call the cleaner.

Have clean clothes for Tom to wear to school tomorrow.

Keep Sam Hill off Corbins' lawn.

Make us some cookies, but not with coconut.

Change the bedding.

Don't spend too much time on the phone. We might be trying to call you to bring us something we forgot.

Don't wash Kathy's T-shirt. She prefers it the way it is.

Write a check for Gerry's music lesson.

If a stranger comes to the door, let him in. The dishwasher broke, and someone will need to fix it.

Love, Gerry and Kathy

Margaret Hill

September 9

I had come to India from our home in Maryland and established a second residence in Hyderabad, near the orphanage where I had adopted my sons. My husband had returned to his job in Maryland while the boys and I waited for notification that our daughter Ghita's papers were processed.

Finally the news arrived that I could proceed to Nagpur and immediately take custody of my daughter. I arranged to travel by air, and then a Hindu temple in the north was bombed by Muslims. All flights were canceled for fear of terrorism.

I decided to travel by train until our hired driver and close friends advised me to abandon my plans. Driving was not safe either.

Gradually, over the months, the tension between the Hindus and Muslims dissolved, and flights to Nagpur resumed. I could hardly contain myself as the moment we had waited for arrived. Out of the crowd, one shining little face stepped forward and said, "Mommy!" It was her first English word, spoken with eyes as big as the universe and enough love to last a lifetime.

Amsheva Miller

watched as she led him by the hand to the bathroom at the airport terminal. He seemed a little bewildered but secure as long as his hand was in hers. She combed his hair and zipped his jacket. He fidgeted and asked, "Where are we going, Mommy? When will we get to ride our plane?"

We sat together on the plane. He became frightened when the jet engines started. He asked many questions about the time, what day it was, how much longer until they got there . . . and she lovingly held his hand and gave him her full attention. I learned she had four children and was on her way to visit one of them.

The hour passed quickly, and soon we had landed. They got off before I did, the mother never realizing how deeply she had touched me. As I watched her lead her husband of 44 years to the baggage claim area, I said a little prayer for myself . . . that I would have enough love and strength to meet whatever challenges came my way, as this extraordinary mother clearly had.

Bobbie Wilkinson

September 11

Mount Pleasant, South Carolina, U.S.A.

September 11 dealt a stunning blow to the American psyche. Local and national news commentators urged us to respond to the call for blood donations. Tuesday night I told my husband, "We've got to go tomorrow."

We couldn't believe what awaited us when we reached our local Red Cross. It might be eight hours before we reached the head of the line. While we waited, I saw the face of America around me.

I saw young and old, women with children, Generation-Xers in T-shirts and tattoos, veterans, people leaning on canes and in wheelchairs, waiting to give what they had.

We were just Americans, doing what we do. We sang to the music from the speakers and we laughed, because Americans are people who love to laugh. We made friends and discovered common ground. Our hearts were broken, but our spirit was roaring back. We had a common purpose and a common goal. We were once again the UNITED States.

Susan Halm, edited by Joyce Schowalter

In 1949, my father had just returned home from the war, but the thrill of his reunion with his family was soon overshadowed. My grandmother had to be hospitalized. The doctors told my father that she needed a blood transfusion immediately or she would not live through the night. The problem was, her blood type was AB-, a very rare type. Not one member of the family was a match, so the doctors gave the family no hope.

My father left the hospital to gather up all the family members to tell Grandmother good-bye. He passed a soldier in uniform hitchhiking home. Though he had no inclination to do a good deed, something pulled him to a stop.

The stranger noticed my father's tears right away and inquired about them. It got very quiet in the car as my father told the story. Then this unidentified soldier showed my father his dog tags, AB-. The soldier told my father to turn the car around and get him to the hospital.

My grandmother lived until 1996. To this day no one in my family knows the soldier's name.

Jeannie Ecke Sowell

Doing a good deed has unimaginable rewards.

September 13

After a long flight from Boston, I finally landed in Houston well after midnight. My friend Scott, who works at a large hotel chain, had held the "sleeping room" for me at another hotel. At 2:45 in the morning the desk clerk ushered me into a room that must have been 2,500 square feet. Scott had "stuck" me in the presidential suite!

On the coffee table was an assortment of beer, and tequila, a bowl of corn chips, a gallon of salsa and two pounds of guacamole.

I called the front desk. "I cannot possibly eat or drink all this stuff. Can you send someone up to help?"

All through the night, security guards, housekeepers, kitchen staff and even the front-desk clerk rotated through the suite to join the feeding frenzy.

As I was preparing for my business meeting, I learned it had been canceled, and the budget for the entire program had been eliminated. Then the bill was slipped under the door.

$1,954!

My heart stopped. But at the bottom were the signatures of all the staff who had joined me and a stamp that read: PAID.

Jim Feldman

*W*hen I became pregnant with our fifth child, we decided to have all four of our children present during the birth of this new baby . . . if they wanted to be.

We explained how we might have to wake them in the middle of the night. We told them they had to be very respectful of what was going on, and if they were uncomfortable to just leave the room and wait nearby. We explained how the baby might not look like what they would expect. They were keen and excited about being there.

We found a doctor who supported and was in full agreement with our unusual family plan, and then the big night finally arrived.

Our kids gasped in awe as the baby's head crowned. Then the full body appeared, and the doctor shouted, "It's a boy!"

The bond between the children and the new baby is phenomenal. There is no rivalry or jealousy. They simply adore him for the special person he is, and all because we invited them, and shared with them, the very special event of Levi's birth.

Dawn and Tim Johnson

September 15

I couldn't wait for my son to talk. Only later did I realize how little control I had over what he'd say and when he'd say it. We had taught our son to be observant; what we hadn't shown him was when and why to keep his observations to himself.

When he was three, he hailed a couple of elderly women. "You'd like my grandmother," he assured them. "She's old, too." Another time he waved away a smoker: "Hey, you're going to die!"

Each time, we'd stammer an apology and sweep Sam off for a chat. At age four, he began to grapple with the notion that words could embarrass or hurt.

At my health club, we passed an acquaintance whose left arm ended just below the shoulder. I smiled, or gritted my teeth as I imagined what Sam might say. As I pulled him along, his eyes widened, but he said nothing.

Later, I complimented Sam on his restraint. "He knows he only has one arm, Mom," he replied, patiently. "I didn't want to hurt his feelings."

By God, he had it! And then....

"Mom? Could we take his picture?"

Maybe we have more work to do.

Barbara Hoffman

It was the third day my husband, Joe, had been in the intensive care unit following his fifth surgery for the removal of most of his remaining small intestine. The surgery took many more hours than expected. Joe was older and weaker, and he wasn't responding.

Two nurses tried repeatedly to get him to cough, open his eyes, move a finger—anything.

Finally, one of them turned to me and said, "Maybe you, as his daughter, could help us." I smiled and said, "I'll be happy to give you personal information, and thank you for the compliment, but I'm his wife of forty-three years, and we're about the same age."

As they were expressing how I looked so young, a little cough came from my husband, and we all turned to stare at him. He didn't open his eyes, but loud and clear he said, "She dyes her hair!"

Donna Parisi

Humor can awaken the soul.

September 17

"Dear Lord, could you please send two angels to protect my daddy?"

I asked my girls to pray this prayer every day while my husband was gone, and I repeated a similar prayer many times throughout the day.

Two weeks after my husband's return from Baghdad, he told a story of how he returned to his trailer after midnight and felt that there was an intruder in his small living quarters. His search revealed nothing, so he prepared for bed. One hour later he was awakened by gunfire. Lying on his belly with his weapon drawn, he was never afraid.

My daughter asked how this was possible.

My husband said that he could feel someone in the room protecting him. Actually, he said, it felt more like two. "Daddy's angels," my daughter said quietly.

Tammy Ross

September 18

*W*hen our daughter Meegan lost her front tooth at the age of six, we found the following note wrapped around the tiny tooth:

Der Tooth Fary. Pleze leve me yor majik wand. I can hep. I want to be a tooth fary too.

Luv Meegan

The "Tooth Fary" left the following note:

You are too young for the job just now, so I cannot give you my wand. But there are some things that you can start to do to prepare yourself for the job:

1) Always do your best in every job that you do.
2) Treat all people as you wish to be treated.
3) Be kind and helpful to others.
4) Always listen carefully whenever people speak to you.

Meegan took the message to heart and carefully followed the instructions, always working to improve as she grew. By the time she was 27, she was top manager of a company.

She told me the company president had one day asked what influences had motivated her.

She replied, "My parents, my teacher and my friends. And, of course, the Tooth Fairy!"

Suzanne Moustakas

September 19

As I approached my fortieth birthday, I was tired all the time, weighed about 200 pounds, and was becoming more and more depressed. I made an appointment to see a doctor.

My blood count was low, my estrogen level was really bad, I was 60 pounds overweight, etc., etc. I started taking what I called my "turning 40 meds" and wanted to start an exercise program. "Not until we get all this other stuff in order," my nurse practitioner said.

Months went by before I was able to start an exercise program. I signed up for kickboxing and Tae Bo and bought all the equipment. By week three, I had worked myself up to a half-hour before I left the building wheezing and decided this wasn't going to work.

Then I had an idea. In college I had been an aerobics instructor, so I thought about getting together with a few friends to work out. I found a space and placed a small classified ad offering FREE aerobics classes to encourage people to keep their fitness resolutions. Seventy people showed up.

So here I am, celebrating one year, forty pounds lighter, energetic and full of self-esteem, and working out with 250 women.

Rita V. Williams

*O*ver the years we have discovered that being sisters and being close does not necessarily mean we agree on everything. Growing up, we differed on many things, but today we agree on what is really important: being sisters.

Two events made us realize the importance of being sisters—our mother's death and her terrible lung cancer. After mother's funeral, hurtful words were spoken by both of us. It went like this.

"It's mine!"

"No, she would have wanted me to have it!"

Months of silence went by while we both cried by ourselves. She made the first offer of reconciliation, which I joyfully accepted.

Then my sister went into the hospital to have a cyst on her leg removed. A routine chest X ray showed one lung full of cancer tumors.

Chemotherapy is holding the disease at bay, and we have come to realize our time together here is fleeting and precious. We don't always agree, of course, but now it goes like this.

"You take it! It's yours."

"No, you take it! It's yours."

Jane Eppinga

September 21

It was the morning of Friday, September 21, 2001. I was walking through the United Airlines terminals at O'Hare International Airport. Copeland's "Appalachian Spring" was playing over the airport sound system.

"Catchy tune, isn't it?" It was the voice of a United pilot. Unsolicited, he turned to me and said, "There are two ways to stop all of this. One is the fact that in my hands I control an extremely powerful piece of equipment, and if I have to, I can cause that plane to have so much turbulence that you couldn't hold down your lunch.

"The second way is when the passengers become fed up," clearly implying the counterattack methods used by passengers on Flight 93.

I was stunned by the power of his words. After welcoming everyone aboard, he repeated his message over the plane's PA system.

Now, I am not a person who advocates violence, but there we were in the face of all that anxiety and fear, and this wonderful captain made us all realize that we need not be passive victims, but that our fate is at least partially in our own hands and his.

Matthew E. Adams

September 22

In 1966, I brought music and reading to the lives of the "educationally deprived" in southwest Virginia.

My first day I noticed the dirtiest child I had ever seen, sitting isolated from the rest. He didn't touch the musical instrument I had given him, but I noticed his fingers moved with the beat of the music.

"Oh, that's just Roscoe," one of the teachers told me. "He just comes to school so he can have a hot meal every day."

The principal at the high school told me his family was infamous in the area. There was incest, alcoholism, mental illness and various other problems in the clan.

When I walked into the classroom for only the second time, there was Roscoe, sitting in the front row, waiting for the music teacher.

As the year progressed, I took clothes to Roscoe, convinced the teacher to help me clean him up and watched as he began to blossom.

Roscoe learned to read, learned his alphabet and numbers, and showed an artistic nature that was superior to most of the other children in the class. He became part of their games at recess and was no longer looked upon as "different."

Sue L. Vaughn

September 23

Every year my birthday followed the same ritual. I would open the door, and my mother would be standing on the step with wind swirling leaves around her feet.

There would be a chill in the air, and in her hands she would hold my birthday gift. It would always be something small and precious, something I had needed for a long time and just never knew it.

I would open this gift with great care, then I would tuck it carefully away with all my heart's possessions.

If my mother could come to me today on my birthday, I would bring her into the warmth of my kitchen. Then we would have a cup of tea. There would be no rush to open my gift, because today I would know that I had already opened it when I opened the front door to find her there.

Christina Keenan

The presence of a loved one is the most important gift a person can receive.

*W*hen my wife Peggy and I quit our jobs to teach in Lima, Peru, most of our colleagues and friends simply thought we were crazy. Then we started hearing the other comment: "We almost quit our jobs and traveled." We knew what we were doing was right.

For over a year, we boiled every drop of water we drank. We dodged rats in the streets during early morning jobs. When earthquakes racked our apartment, we huddled in the doorway, listening to the prayers screamed in Spanish outside.

Bu we also slept in ancient ruins while hiking the Inca Trail, climbed mountains and jumbled glaciers, and soaked in natural hot springs.

After 18 months overseas, we arrived home with no money. But our riches included a shelf of ragged guide-books, a trunk of well-worn maps, two minds filled with memories and no urge to say, "We almost did that."

Steve Gardiner

*Follow your wishes and dreams today
so that tomorrow you don't have to say,
"I wish I did that."*

September 25

We arrived at the hospital to find Dad exhausted and weak, but his smile was as sure as ever. It was another bout of pneumonia. My husband and I stayed the weekend, but had to return to our jobs. Local relatives would take care of him, but I longed to be able to let him know that we cared too, even when we weren't with him.

Then I remembered a family tradition I initiated when our children were small. As I tidied up Dad's kitchen and made up a bed for him downstairs, I began writing notes. Some were practical: "Dad, I froze the casserole that was in the fridge." Some expressed my love: "I hope you sleep well in your new bed." Most notes were left downstairs, where he would be confined for several weeks until he regained strength.

We stayed in touch by phone, but our notes were a tangible reminder of our love and concern for him. Several weeks later I asked Dad how he was doing. He said, "I just found your note under my upstairs pillow." My note read: "Dad, if you have found this note, you must be feeling better. We are so glad!"

Emily Chase

*I*f I were lucky in this lifetime, I would learn the art of letting go.

I would start with the bathroom scale. Next would be my watch. Perfection, next big hit. Let the housework pile up and invite lots of friends over.

Next, get rid of that worry dance I do. The health of my husband, safety of my children, not enough money, being alone, tax collectors, termites.

I would sit on the beach with my friends and eat junky hot dogs. I would take long walks with my husband.

Sometimes I would sit quietly on my porch and listen to the birds for hours. I would surround myself with people who love nature, laughter and dessert.

I would spend my time living large and doing nothing.

I would sit back and enjoy the journey.

Avis Drucker

**To enjoy the journey of living,
you have to learn the art of letting go.**

September 27

When she was 35, Caren suffered a brain hemorrhage. Doctors warned it could happen again. Especially if she got pregnant.

She and Eric had been looking forward to starting a family. Since her health problems weren't genetic, Caren suggested they try to find a surrogate. They passed the word through the family, and on Caren's thirty-sixth birthday, Eric's sister announced she would be honored to carry their baby for them.

Caren and Eric accompanied Jan to every doctor's appointment. The women shopped together for maternity outfits, and Caren celebrated every new milestone. In the delivery room, Caren and Eric stood on either side of Jan, holding her hands and helping her with her breathing. They named him Blake Jan, in honor of the woman who had made it all possible.

"How can I ever thank you enough for what you've done?" Caren sobbed as she and Eric prepared to take their baby home.

"Enjoy your baby," came Jan's simple, heartfelt reply.

Heather Black

*O*nce upon a time, my friend Joan believed the childhood chant, "Sticks and stones may break my bones, but words can never hurt me." Then she grew up.

As an adult, she tipped the scales at well over 500 pounds. Joan has learned how to avoid the cutting remarks people make: She stays home.

But with their twenty-fifth wedding anniversary approaching, her husband planned a romantic evening out for the two of them. Joan decided to sew a dressy new blouse for their celebration.

The restaurant was perfect, but the patrons weren't. Joan managed to ignore the blunt comments and rude stares, but when a young girl headed toward their table, Joan cringed.

Joan held her breath while a tiny hand gently stroked her sleeve. "You're so pretty in that top." Then the little girl smiled and walked back to her seat.

That single compliment changed Joan's life. "Now, when people mutter behind my back, I'm sure the words everyone whispers . . . are flattering," Joan says. "That's all I hear—now. Only compliments. Words that can never hurt me."

Carol McAdoo Rehme

You can hear only compliments
if that's what you choose to hear.

September 29

My work in developing a rural pottery project in Nicaragua led me up the steep, rocky trail to Los Chaguites, a brittle, sun-baked settlement usually labeled "inaccessible." It was on my first trip that I met Doña Pilar and her family. When I pulled out my camera to photograph several pieces of pottery, they insisted the photo would be much nicer with people in it. I willingly obliged.

A few weeks later, I returned to conduct a pottery workshop. Doña Pilar came out to greet me. *"Y la foto?"* she asked hopefully. I pulled the photograph from my backpack.

After a long lapse of silence, Doña Pilar pointed to a short, gray-haired grandmotherly woman and asked timidly, "Is this me?"

I realized that Doña Pilar clearly had no idea what she looked like. When I asked if she had ever owned a mirror, she said yes, but it had broken. "I know who I am inside," she replied, "and that's what I see every day."

Jane E. Hall

*M*y oldest was small and her sister quite tall, so folks often thought they were twins. They loved sleeping together under a big green quilt—my grandmother Nana's gift to me on the day of my marriage. For most of their childhood, my girls dragged that quilt everywhere. When they entered their teens, along went the quilt.

College and marriage finally parted my girls, ironically, on the same day. As they walked out of their room for the last time, I noticed loving fingers giving a last caress to their beloved quilt.

When they were gone, with firm resolve, I took a deep breath and cut the old cover in half. The following Christmas I gave each daughter her share, freshly adorned with dotted-swiss ruffles.

Now, whenever I visit their homes, I joyfully cover my grandbabies with Nana's sun-dried quilt.

Lynne Zielinski

October 1

*L*ast summer we were planning a large family reunion. Finally, we'd be able to gather all our wonderful grandchildren together.

Our youngest son arrived with our youngest granddaughter. My daughter-in-law, well-meaning as she was, pushed three-year-old Marie toward us. "Give Grandma and Grandpa kisses hello," she said.

Marie looked panicked and ducked behind her mom's legs.

Throughout the reunion Marie continued to hide whenever her mom asked her to give us a kiss. As my son prepared to leave for the airport, I told my daughter-in-law that I needed to say a special good-bye to Marie.

I bent over and stared right into her eyes—long and hard—until finally I had to stand up.

"What was that all about?" asked my son.

"Our eyeballs kissed," I said.

Slowly, a grin split Marie's face from ear to ear and she laughed. Then she ran to me and gave me a big hug. "Silly Gramma," she whispered. "I'll miss you."

Angela D'Valentine

October 2

I first met Sheba when I was a third-grade student. She was a seven-week-old kitten in a pet-shop window. Through the glass, we concluded that we were made for each other.

Unfortunately, Mom and Dad didn't think much of my plans. To them a kitten was something you can get for free at any barn, not something you had to pay two dollars and fifty cents for.

However, after a lot of kid whining and with a chunk of "birthday money," Sheba was mine. I was an instant hit with her, and the feeling was mutual.

Through junior high, high school and college she remained a close feline friend and was largely responsible for my deciding to pursue a career as a veterinarian.

Sheba was 22 years old on the day I opened my veterinary hospital for cats only. But Mom and Dad brought her to see me for another reason. She had become quite ill, and I could see the situation was hopeless. We had the last of our long conversations as she fell gently asleep in my arms.

Michael A. Obenski

October 3

"I'm sorry, Mrs. Coe. The test was negative." I'd known I wasn't pregnant for the last week and a half. This had been our last in vitro fertilization attempt. I was numb.

What did I do to deserve this?

So we'd adopt. But since the agency hadn't placed any babies in the last year, we'd have to find a baby ourselves.

One day the phone rang. A young woman wanted to give us a baby. Ultrasound showed us we were going to become parents of a perfect little girl.

Then the most unlikely of unlikelies happened. Another woman wanted to give us a baby boy, born just that morning. The papers were signed within hours, and we were parents.

But what about the baby girl? We decided to take her, too. So, exactly one month later, we became parents again. As inexperienced parents of two tiny babies, the next few months were harder than we'd ever imagined. But today, a door opens to a nursery school classroom, and two pairs of legs come running toward me. "Mommy! Mommy!" I kneel, my arms open wide.

What did I do to deserve this?

Cynthia Coe

*A*s we prepared to leave our family get-together, my cousin Doug called to us to wait.

"You forgot your sourdough bread, and here is your starter jar so you can make it." He pushed through the window a glass jar containing a white, gooey blob. "Here's the recipe to make it. Put it in the refrigerator when you get home, but don't forget it. Like friendships, you have to tend it."

"You know I'm too busy to bake."

"Make time," he shot back. "It's important to spend time with your friends, to have fun."

At his funeral, it was evident that he had done just that. People from all walks of life came to mourn his tragic death. He had been right. You can't let a hectic life keep you from enjoying life—and your friends.

Several days later, the delicious scent of baking bread wafted through the house. I picked up the phone and called my neighbor. "I know that I've been neglecting my friends," I confessed, "so how about coming over for some sourdough bread? We need to catch up."

Debra Ayers Brown

You can't let a hectic life keep you from enjoying life—and your friends.

October 5

> *Twenty years from now you will be*
> *more disappointed by the things*
> *that you didn't do than by the ones*
> *you did do. So throw off the bowlines.*
> *Sail away from the safe harbor.*
> *Catch the trade winds in your sails.*
> *Explore. Dream. Discover.*

Mark Twain

_____
_____
_____
_____
_____
_____
_____
_____
_____
_____
_____

*M*y six-year-old granddaughter, Caitlynd, and I had stopped at a donut shop for a muffin. As we were going out the door, a young teenage boy was coming in. He had a tuft of blue spiked hair on top of his head, one of his nostrils was pierced, and attached to a hoop that ran through the hold was a chain that draped across his face. He held a skateboard under one arm and a basketball under the other.

Caitlynd stopped in her tracks and opened the door as wide as it would go. His response was a gracious, "Thank you very much."

I was ready for a grandmotherly talk about freedom of self-expression, but as it turned out, the only thing Caitlynd had noticed was the fact that his arms were full. "He woulda had a hard time to open the door."

In the future, I hope to get down on her level and raise my sights.

Terri McPherson

To raise your sights,
you need to get down on a child's level.

October 7

E ve Jesson had been widowed at 70 and had a stroke at age 74. Her daughter urged Mrs. Jesson to join their household, but she gently refused and moved into a nursing home where I was a caregiver.

It was difficult for us to find her a suitable companion to share the two-person bedroom. Margaret Gravelle seemed a more suitable roommate than many others.

Mrs. Jesson had to remind Margaret of mealtimes and guide her to the dining room. Margaret could not grasp the notion that only one of the closets was hers, and sometimes put on Mrs. Jesson's clothes. Margaret also woke her several times during the night when she got confused.

The day came when we arranged to admit a lady we thought would be a better companion for Mrs. Jesson. We told her we would have to arrange to move Margaret first.

Later in the day, Mrs. Jesson came down to my desk. "Maybe I'm meant to look out for Margaret. I can give her some of the comfort my family gives me. Leave Margaret in my room. It won't take that much effort to watch over her a bit."

Marian Lewis

However long you live, there is always one more task that needs to be completed. That's what keeps you going.

*A*s everything unraveled on our 25-year marriage, I felt huge relief that our only child was 20 by that time. I had said to my daughter and her dad that the nature and quality of their relationship from that point on would be up to them. I would neither facilitate nor interfere.

Just when I was congratulating myself on our having handled things in a way that left her relatively unscathed, she told me she was dreading her college graduation. "Every time you see Dad or talk about him, you cry and feel sad. It makes me not want to go through graduation."

"I know it wasn't easy to say that," I managed to mutter. "It's six months until graduation. I promise you that on that weekend, we'll be fine."

And we were. That's when I knew my choice to spend time with him during the months after her sad confrontation had been worthwhile. By "practicing" being cordial and friendly, I had moved beyond the automatic response of tears. And it wasn't long before I realized that forgiveness had crept into my heart. A teacher once said, "Forgiving may help the forgiver more than the forgiven." She was right.

Susan Carver Williams

October 9

*W*hen Cori was six, her father and I divorced. Not long afterward, I fell into a life of addiction. Sickness was all I could offer her at the time, yet she never wavered in her love for me. Cori died on her birthday, one of eight teenagers who died in a head-on collision on a sparkling summer day.

It would be a neat and tidy story to say that Cori's death sobered me up. Instead, I redoubled my drug taking and pursued several more years of addiction before I finally sought treatment.

One of the stops on my journey was the coroner's office where I had last seen Cori. That she had died quickly was important for me to know. That she had not been drinking meant a great deal to me.

Wanting to feel her presence again, I went to the accident site. As I stood praying, I heard a faint crunch under one foot. There, sticking out of the dirt, were Cori's rosary beads.

Chris Lloyd

I was deep in thought, working on editing a draft, when my five-year-old son, Jake, came into my office. When I finished my thought, I glanced over at him. "Yes, Jake? What do you need, honey?"

"I want to make a 'pottment," he replied.

"What do you mean—an appointment?" I asked him.

His lips quivered, and his words gushed forth. "So you can talk to me, and write about me, and play with me, and make yellow sticky notes that say Jake on 'em . . . and so you won't ever forget me."

I reached for my son and pulled him close.

Long after he was tucked in bed that night, I began a new project—a short picture book that consisted of nothing more than photos, captions and a simple story line.

The next morning I called Jake to me. He began flipping through the pages of photos of our special times as I read the words aloud. "Wow!" Jake said. "You're a real writer, huh, Mom?"

I said, "I guess so."

"I know what writers do," claimed Jake. "They make people feel good with words. That's cool!"

Valerie Hutchins

October 11

*L*ittle Lucy (at least that's what we'll call her) had never been to kindergarten before. She was thrilled by the activities, the children, the classroom—and especially the noise. Her parents were deaf, and every conversation was conducted in sign language. Now Lucy was getting to talk!

As the holidays approached, dozens of tiny hands were traced onto colorful paper. Hundreds of tiny fingers were cut out, and the handprints were taped on the door. Lucy loved the tracing and the cutting. She worked on it at home and brought the best hand of all to take to her teacher.

"Do you like it?" Lucy asked eagerly.

"Yes, honey, but there are some fingers missing. Did something happen?"

It was obvious that the thumb, index finger and pinky finger had been cut with perfection. The other two, however, had been cut off at the palm.

"Yes, teacher, I wanted to give you my best hand—the one that says 'I love you.'"

And that's exactly what it did say—in sign language.

Suzanne Boyce

**Communicate your feelings
in whatever language you know.**

*S*ophomore year of high school had been difficult for me. Being at a new school is challenging for most kids. It didn't help having to monitor my diabetes and live with other health-related issues.

The highlight of my day was choir class. Half the choir was made up of girls with special needs, and there I felt accepted.

One day the entire school gathered for the Holiday Wish Fairy Assembly. I sat back and waited for it to be over. *What a dumb assembly!* I thought.

Soon, all eyes were on Elizabeth, a girl from my choir. "My wish today is that I could give Jenna Mitchell a present."

I rose to my feet and walked to the stage with the entire school watching.

"I want to thank Jenna for being my best friend at school," she began, "and I want to give her this necklace."

Extending her hand toward mine, Elizabeth gave me a small gold box. As the students watched, I thanked Elizabeth and gave her a hug.

Jenna Mitchell

October 13

There are only two ways to live your life.
One is as though nothing is a miracle.
The other is as though everything is a miracle.

Albert Einstein

_____

_____

_____

_____

_____

_____

_____

_____

_____

_____

_____

_____

_____

_____

October 14

I love to give and receive presents. One day my grandson, Justin, sent me $6.30. I thought about that for a couple of days and then called him.

I asked, "Why did you send Grandma six dollars and thirty cents?"

Justin told me that I always did such nice things for him that he wanted to give me everything he had.

I knew in my heart that I would never again receive a gift given with such pure and innocent love.

Irene (Seida) Carlson

A gift from a child is given with love.

October 15

𝓘 am a single mother of two. When my oldest child started school, I was like all mothers: I felt as if someone just snatched him from me, and I would never have his full attention and dependence again.

I had a lot of time to share with my youngest child, who is three years younger. I had him at my side tugging at my shirt strings for three years. Where I went he went.

One morning I came home from work, exhausted, changed out of my uniform and slipped into the car to get errands done before getting a few hours of sleep. My last stop was at Kmart where I was looking for a red T-shirt to match the shorts I had bought Jeremy for school.

I spotted the perfect shirt, turned around to tell him, and he was gone. I looked for him, called his name, but he never answered. I was panicking, screaming his name. By this time, a policeman was asking me questions. "Ma'am, what was he wearing?"

I started telling him, then turned red with embarrassment. "I am so sorry," I exclaimed. "He started kindergarten today."

Patsy Hughes

October 16

*D*eep in the mire of love, my younger sister was gushing about an all-important date—she and Mr. Be-All-End-All's first anniversary of dating. She was in a state—would he remember, would he forget? Of course, he was going to forget. He was a guy.

As was my custom, I headed home the following Friday that, as the fates would have it, was *the* day. I stopped by the high school and talked with my sister. No card, no acknowledgment. She was crushed.

I sought out the tarnished hero. I mentioned that I knew the importance of the day and that I happened to have a lovely arrangement of flowers sitting in my vehicle. A lifeline was thrown to him.

That evening my reenchanted sister told how he had asked her to go for a ride with him to his parents' house where he had a bouquet of absolutely beautiful flowers waiting for her.

That was eight years ago. On August 1, my sister and Mr. Be-All-End-All celebrated their third wedding anniversary. My part in their romance was miniscule, but it made my sister happy and that's the only thing that matters.

Chera Lee Bammerlin

Never underestimate the power of love.

October 17

On a weekend off, my husband and I headed for the Cubs ballpark via the train. As we arrived at the final station, the conductor hustled us to the door. On the way, I glimpsed some people huddled around a man lying limply in his seat. I told the conductor I was a nurse and offered to help.

"I don't need a nurse," he snapped. "I need a medic!"

I abruptly elbowed my way through the crowd. "Help me sit him up," I instructed the bystanders, as I loosened his collar and tie. I quickly did a jaw thrust and tilted his head to the side. With a wadded tissue from my pocket, I cleared his mouth and throat, and a thump on the shoulder caused him to take in a big breath of air. Within seconds, his color changed and his eyes opened.

As I returned to my husband, I stared at the conductor. He stammered, "I guess a nurse is what I needed after all."

Barbara A. Brady

Professionalism under stress earns respect.

October 18

In our kindergarten class, we constantly encouraged children to recognize and accept strengths in themselves and others. One of our strongest class rules was, "We will say only kind things to each other."

One day the children were seated on the floor eagerly relating experiences about springtime when Michael raised his hand, as he often did. But Michael couldn't speak. I recognized him each time he raised his hand and gave him time to respond. After a few minutes, I would respond as if he had. "Michael, that was a good try."

When Michael raised his hand again this day, to our great surprise, he spoke! The energy in the room was overwhelming. One of my class angels, Nicole, spoke first, "That was a great wrong answer!" The class immediately stood and gave him a standing ovation.

Bonnie Block

October 19

*M*y husband, Serge, and I faced each other across the pristine sheets of the hospital bed. The bogeyman of cancer was literally going to change the face of our lives.

Four-year-old Kate was happily cranking the foot of the bed up and down. The first of Daddy's weeklong overnights in the hospital was an adventure to her.

A nurse popped her head in the door. "Time to go. Visiting hours are over."

Kate stopped cranking the bed, took a quick look under it, then picked up her backpack from the chair and unzipped it. She carefully lifted out Mishka, a stuffed bear that had sat at the foot of Serge's bed while he was growing up, and had been spruced up and given to Kate. "He's a guard bear," she said, and he always slept at the foot of her bed.

Kate whispered something in Mishka's ear, hugged him tightly for a minute and then put him in her father's arms. "He'll protect you in the night, Daddy," she said, "whenever monsters come."

Anne Metikosh

October 20

As the principal of the largest high school in Oklahoma City, my role in the baccalaureate service was minimal. I helped students pin collars on their robes, quieted the nervous jitters and supervised as they lined up for this most important event.

Finally, all was in readiness, and I slid silently into a back pew. The program began normally with a routine of introductions and speeches. Then came the senior solo —one of the most coveted parts of the ceremony.

One of our young ladies walked proudly to the lectern to sing "His Eye Is on the Sparrow." However, as she began, she stumbled through the first verse, and tears started running down her face. Suddenly, from the back of the church, the song echoed from another voice. Her older sister calmly walked down the center aisle of the church, keeping her eyes on her sister, and she continued to sing along. Side by side, they sang triumphantly, the original singer buoyed by the love and courage of her family member, until the song was finished.

Rita Billbe

October 21

*The greatest happiness of life is the conviction
that we are loved—loved for ourselves,
or rather, loved in spite of ourselves.*

Victor Hugo

_____

_____

_____

_____

_____

_____

_____

_____

_____

_____

_____

_____

_____

_____

*W*hen I decided to become a comedy writer, I wanted to study the profession. So I studied Bob Hope—the joke forms, wording, rhythm, arrangement of gags in a routine and so on. With this technique, Bob Hope and his writers became my mentors.

It worked. I began writing for local comics, then national comics. Then it worked even better. Bob Hope called and asked me to do some gags for him for the Academy Awards.

I wrote a few hundred gags about current movies, celebrities—anything that would apply to the Oscars. Mr. Hope did 10 of my jokes on the telecast, and I was thrilled. I've been writing for Bob Hope ever since.

There were two valuable lessons in this experience that all writers can learn and draw inspiration from.

One: There is effort involved in making any dream come true. Dreams are powerful, but only when they're reinforced by research, study and effort.

Two: If you do the work, you'll reach your goals.

Gene Perret

Dreams are powerful, but only when they are reinforced by research, study and effort.

October 23

We were shocked when the adoption agency said we were matched for a baby boy three months after we had completed the paperwork. "Is the nursery ready?" asked a business associate. Well, not exactly. We had nothing for the baby. The would-be nursery was water damaged and very badly in need of rewiring, new walls, a new ceiling and floor.

We worked during the day and like mad by night. Friends, family and sometimes even complete strangers showed up with used baby furniture, clothes and a host of other necessities. We had almost completed the room by the time my husband and I boarded the flight.

Three weeks and a long airplane ride later, we walked through the door of our home with our son. While we were gone, the nursery had been finished and the refrigerator stocked with several meals for us.

Friends and family came throughout the next few days to see our son and bring items we needed. Reflecting on our first few hours home as a family, we realized that we had already been part of a caring extended family, larger than we could have ever imagined.

Cynthia Hummel

Emergency-room personnel transported him to the cardiac floor. Definitely an untouchable!

One of the true marks of a leader is to do the unthinkable. To tackle the impossible. It was Bonnie, the head nurse, who said, "I want this patient myself."

As she donned her latex gloves and proceeded to bathe this huge, filthy man, her heart almost broke. Then, on a whim she said, "We don't have time for back rubs much in hospitals these days, but I bet one would really feel good. It would help you relax your muscles and start to heal."

His thick, scaly, ruddy skin told a story of an abusive lifestyle. The finale—warmed lotion and baby powder. Almost laughable—such a contrast on this huge, rugged surface. As he rolled over onto his back, tears rolled down his cheek. "No one has touched me for years." His chin trembled. "Thank you. I am healing."

Naomia Rhode

A simple touch can start the healing.

October 25

Someone special, a friend so true,
Exactly the same, yet different from you;
She knows your thoughts without a word,
Understands your feelings before they're heard;
May drift apart but remains near,
In her heart she holds you dear;
Your secrets safe, your faults untold,
A bond of trust she will uphold;
So cherish her as she does you,
For remember you are a sister, too.

Lisa Baillargeon

Every morning our dog, Brownie, was let out by the first person who got up. When we called him back in, he'd usually come running … but not on this particular Sunday. We called and coaxed, but Brownie was nowhere to be found. We gave up and headed off to church.

We got settled in, with Mother at the organ. As the minister began his sermon, we kids heard a scratching at the church door, which was followed by the plaintive sound of a lonely dog howling. Only one dog in the neighborhood made that sound.

The minister signaled the usher to shoo the dog away, but he was not quick enough for Brownie, who bounded in and strolled up the aisle to where Mother sat at the organ. Then he just plopped down and sat quietly.

There were many Sundays when Brownie repeated his demonstrations of religious piety and family loyalty. And since Brownie lived to be 19 years old, quite a few preachers got used to having that little brown dog interrupt their Sunday services.

Evelyn Olson

October 27

In today's society, it seems the major criteria for receiving megadollar salaries seem to be determined by how much the audience will pay to watch the performer achieve.

Then why choose teaching for a career?

My family was gathered for a leisurely summer barbecue. Dessert was being served when the phone rang. My husband handed it to me, saying, "They're looking for Bonnie Block."

"Is this the Bonnie Block who used to teach kindergarten?" the voice on the other end of the line asked.

"Yes!" I exclaimed.

"I am Danielle—Danielle Russ. I was in your kindergarten class. I'm graduating from high school this year, and I have been trying to find you. I wanted you to know what a difference you made in my life."

She proceeded to give details of how I made that difference. My influence wasn't limited to kindergarten. When she needed a coach to help her meet a challenge, "I pictured you praising and encouraging me all the way."

Why choose teaching?

The pay is great!

Bonnie Block

When choosing a career, consider that the pay doesn't always come in the form of money.

October 28

For one human being to love another;
that is perhaps the most difficult of all
our tasks, the ultimate, the last test
and proof, the work for which
all other work is but preparation.

Rainer Maria Rilke

_____

_____

_____

_____

_____

_____

_____

_____

_____

_____

_____

_____

_____

_____

October 29

Karen was born with a debilitating condition, and at the age of one year, she suffered a heart attack and was clinically dead for one hour, resulting in harm to her brain. She has grown to be a very beautiful and inspirational young lady, but the greatest fear in her life has been Santa Claus.

Because of the lyric in a particular Christmas song, she has always imagined this big, red-clad, hairy-faced man watching her as she is sleeping.

Karen recently began having these dreams again in quite a severe manner, so her mother looked straight into her eyes and said, "THERE IS NO SANTA CLAUS! MOMMY HAS ALWAYS BEEN SANTA CLAUS!"

The next day at school, Karen looked so disturbed that her teacher asked her what the problem was.

"I am very worried about my mom." When the teacher asked her why, she answered in an equally serious voice, "She thinks she's Santa Claus!"

Brian Locke

A nearly full moon hangs low on the horizon. My footsteps stir the fallen leaves. I'm 10 years old and responsible enough to use matches unsupervised to light a pumpkin I carved by myself with a real knife. I'll even be trick-or-treating with friends and not parents for the first time in my life.

Twenty-five years later, a nearly full moon hangs low on the horizon on a Halloween evening. I'm in a different house in a different state, but the smells are the same. As usual, I am the self-appointed lighter-of-pumpkins, and this year my own children are old enough to be interested in my ritual. "When will we be big enough to do it?" one of my three-year-olds wants to know.

"Maybe when you're ten," I say, remembering.

Pretty soon we're shrieking, laughing, howling, cavorting in the mist and the moonlight. "Mommy! Look how big we are!"

And they, newly big, and I, newly little, dance on in the shadows of our common ground, intoxicated on the smell of scorched pumpkin.

Karen C. Driscoll

October 31

If you have spell-checked, rewritten at least 20 times, followed guidelines, submitted to the appropriate market and spelled the editor's name correctly, you could be the lucky one to hear from him by phone. So be ready.

We were still on the ranch my first time. I was filling the water tanks in my chicken coop when the jingle came from the barn. I bolted the door, latched it behind me and 11 rings later grabbed the phone.

"Hello," said the voice on the line. "This is Philip Osborne from the *Reader's Digest*. We'd like to reprint your story that appeared in *Arizona* magazine."

By the time I found Bill out on "the north forty," it was late afternoon, but I had to tell someone. That's when I remembered the hose. I dashed to the coop and lifted the latch. The door flew open, and a four-foot tidal wave of straw, feathers, manure, chicken feed and half-drowned chickens flooded the barnyard. No eggs that month! But *Reader's Digest* bought my story.

Penny Porter

*If you've been working hard,
don't be surprised when success
calls—be prepared.*

had said good-bye to my husband, Joe, so often, but this time was different. We now had our first child.

On Joe's last evening at home, I bathed little Joey, got him into his sleeper and was heading to the bedroom when Joe gently lifted the baby from my arms. He wanted to tuck Joey in tonight.

When a half hour went by and he had not come back, I tiptoed to the baby's room and peeked in.

Sitting in the rocking chair, moving slowly back and forth, was my husband, stifling quiet sobs. His pained eyes met mine, and after a moment he mumbled, "I just can't put him down."

Joey is six now, and he has a four-year-old brother. There have been many farewells since that night, yet my military hero still fights back tears when it's time to leave and give his boys that last, long hug good-bye.

Julie Angelo

November 2

*I*n my grandmother's small kitchen, I watched her scurry back and forth from stove to sink, wiping, straightening . . . Two days before, my grandfather and the love of her life for 58 years had died.

Suddenly, her movements slowed, then she reached behind the toaster and picked up a small vase of cheap plastic flowers. She wiped them off with her towel, then placed the faded arrangement on the tiny table. "I can put my flowers anywhere I want now," she said.

Only days away from her eightieth birthday, she was abut to embark on a journey that would be painfully lonely for a while, but that would eventually lead her to discover the woman she'd left at the altar 58 years ago.

It has been four years since my grandfather passed away, and since then I'm amazed at the woman my grandmother has become. This journey has changed her. Her house is filled with colorful things. Her clothing has become bright and busy. She belongs to a pinochle club and walks three miles a day with her exercise buddies.

She still misses my grandfather, but now she is just doing what comes naturally. Living.

Christie Craig

Do what comes naturally.

*A*fter I had spent a weeklong vigil at the hospital with an ill child, I was not thrilled to see four cars lined up in our driveway. The house was a colossal mess.

"What are you doing home so soon?" my friend Judie called from the kitchen. "We thought we'd be long gone before you got home." She walked toward me and gave me a hug.

Was this my house? Was I dreaming? Everything looked so clean.

Suddenly, more voices, more hugs. Lorraine had ironed a mountain of clothes; Regina had vacuumed and dusted; Joan had brought order out of the chaos in all four bedrooms.

"You rest a while, Virelle," Joan said firmly. "Here's your dinner for tonight—there are more meals in the freezer."

After my friends left, I wandered from room to room. I found beautiful floral arrangements in every room . . . and little wrapped gifts on each bed.

In the living room I found a note under a vase filled with peonies. I was to have come home and found it as their only identity: "The Love Squad was here."

Virelle Kidder

November 4

This spring is my sister's fortieth birthday. That means my fortieth can't be far behind. Since my sister is only 18 months older than I am, I followed a year behind St. Vicki.

As the years went by, the 18-month gulf that separated us closed. Vicki was a voracious and indiscriminate reader. What she read set the scene for our dolls. When we packed them away, we shared boyfriends, makeup, accessories and clothes. The boyfriends we were generous with, but we got pretty vicious over the rest. Our most memorable battles were reserved for a black velvet choker, a mink hair bow, a pearlized snood and a tube of Bonne Belle white-white.

My sister has become my dearest friend, and today I am ashamed of the names I called her and the fits I pitched. All the same, I can't help gloating that she'll be 40 before I will.

If we should live so long, I'll give her a mink hair bow for her eightieth birthday.

Rebecca Christian

I was 41 years old and didn't know how to tell Mum, who had survived the Great Depression, that I was buying an old Volkswagen convertible. I drove home with the top down and parked it squarely in the drive. I helped my mother out of her chair and supported her frail body as we walked to the door.

"Oh, my Lord . . . ," she paused. "What a cute little jalopy! Can we go for a ride?"

She was hooked after the first mile. "Doesn't this make you feel young?" And in my mind's eye, I saw a truly beautiful young woman, not a fragile, ailing 76-year-old. That first week I purchased a heated lap blanket. I would bundle up Mum, toss the blanket over her, and we'd be off. "What a great contraption this is," she'd say with a smile in her voice. "It makes me feel so alive."

Climbing into that little rig enriched the last two years of our lives together. Now my first and last ride of the convertible season is always taken alone. I drop the ragtop and as I drive off, I hear her words in the air beside me: "What a great contraption this is. . . ."

Dorothy Raymond Gilchrest

Doing something simple with someone you care about can create lasting memories.

November 6

*Kindness is the golden chain
by which society is bound together.*

Goethe

_____

_____

_____

_____

_____

_____

_____

_____

_____

_____

_____

_____

_____

_____

_____

hadn't seen my husband in almost six months, and I had to look my best. So off we went to Wal-Mart, where I told everyone within earshot that my husband was coming home from deployment.

We looked through the clothes racks and found outfits for the girls. I was another story. As my daughters delivered their usual "you never buy yourself anything" routine, I looked at the tags and gasped. There was no way I could afford this, so I led my daughters out of the store, explaining our financial limitations.

As we wandered out, a woman walked up to me and handed me a piece of paper. It was a note thanking my husband and me, and blessing us both. Included were three $20 bills.

Jilleen Kesler

November 8

While shopping at a toy store, I came upon a little girl who was looking through Barbie dolls. She had a roll of money clamped in her hand, and each time she saw one she liked, she asked her father if she had enough money to buy it. He usually said "yes,'" but she would keep going through the ritual.

Soon she stopped to watch a boy who was also shopping with his father and kept picking up Pokémon video games. Each time he picked one up, his father shook his head "no."

The boy gave up and chose what looked like a book of stickers. The little girl ran to the Pokémon games, picked one up and got in the checkout line after speaking with her father. The little boy and his father got in line behind me.

After the toy was paid for, the little girl handed it back to the cashier and whispered something to her. As the boy and his father came up, the cashier rang up his purchases and said, "Congratulations, you are my hundredth customer today, and you win a prize!"

Sharon Palmer

*G*oing back to college full-time as a single parent of two had been a difficult choice. But I didn't want to be a welfare mom. Yet without emotional and family support, I had found this to be a journey of being alone, feeling alone and doing it alone. Tonight it hit me all at once. It was too difficult to pay all the bills, take care of the children, study for exams.

My cries must have woken my son because he appeared before me, his eyes filled with concern. "I just find it hard sometimes to take care of you guys and go to college at the same time," I said. My voice broke, "Just tired, I guess."

He came closer and said very quietly, "God made the whole world, Mom. And he's a single parent."

"P.J., that's wonderful! I'm going to put that saying on—just everything!"

After exams were over, I made good on my promise. With the help of a friend, I ordered one thousand coffee mugs; I had them printed with the words, "God Is a Single Parent, Too!" and handed them out to all the single parents I knew.

Tina Fenech

November 10

"Cookie," Papa said, "I've read or told you a story almost every night for six years. Now it's your turn. Tell me a story, and I'll write it down."

So I told him about the time Mama and I visited Grandma Cook's farm when I was four years old, and a big red rooster pecked my big toe with his beak and started after me. I chased him away with a broom, and Mama put medicine on my toes.

Three weeks went by. Papa read to me or told me a story every night, but he didn't seem as happy as he used to be. One night he seemed like his old self. He showed me a newspaper, and there in black letters I recognized my name: Myrtle Cook. He had sent in my story and they had printed it.

A few days later Papa didn't come home. Mama told me they were getting a divorce, and he was moving away. I never saw him again.

I would have grown up thinking Papa didn't love me except for that wonderful thing he did—sending my story to get published.

Cookie Potter

*W*hen you're a child, a sister is a wonderful playmate. When the teen years approach, sisters share one thing in common: fighting.

As pimples give way to engagement rings, sisters share a late-night soda and their dreams, the dividing of the lingerie drawer, the solemnity of the wedding march and the good-bye tears to a chapter of life that has ended.

When buggies and basketballs begin to fill their lives, sisters hold each other close when happiness is overwhelming or grief overpowering.

Sisters can be aunts, wives, mothers or grandmothers, but if your life has been truly blessed, a sister can be your friend.

Alice Collins

If you have a sister who can be your friend, you are truly blessed.

November 12

In the gray light of early morning I'm lost at the computer, focusing hard on today's writing goal. The door scrapes open, and my three-year-old granddaughter breaks my concentration. Jessica pushes the door shut behind her, crawls into my chair and stands up behind me. My fingers go back to the keys. She peers over my shoulder.

Bored with the lack of action on the screen, she lifts my hair. Then, using both hands, she scoops my tousled hair completely over my head. She holds her breath a moment, eyes wide, then dissolves into giggles.

So do I, and that's the end of my writing session for today. Total production: two paragraphs, one unusable.

Funny how the things we love most require some tithe or sacrifice. Chocolate is full of fat and calories. Technology makes life easier, but complicates at the same time. I can't wait for my granddaughter and her family to visit, but when they do, I have to get up in the middle of the night to get my writing done.

Marcia Preston

The things we love most require some sacrifice.

Her world had shattered with the divorce. Her part-time job provided little income and fewer benefits. With no financial support, she had finally lost the house.

At wit's end, Karen managed to rent a cramped camper at the local RV park for herself and five-year-old Joshua. It was only a little better than living out of their car.

One evening after she had sent her son outside to play, she heard voices outside the window.

"Say, Josh, don't you wish you had a real home?" asked the campground manager.

"We already have a real home," Josh said. "It's just that we don't have a house to put it in."

Carol McAdoo Rehme

November 14

Since my husband and I had chosen not to learn the sex of our first child, we decided we would ask the sex of our second child at the seven-month ultrasound. We already had a happy, healthy four-year-old son, and although I kept telling myself that it didn't really matter, secretly I longed for a daughter.

The morning of my ultrasound, I was a nervous wreck. The tech began to describe everything as normal and then, a dramatic pause, "I can definitely tell ... it's a boy."

I am human enough to admit that I was disappointed at first. Then something happened that changed my perspective for the good. Our dearest friends who were in the same stage of pregnancy called to say they were experiencing complications. We cried and prayed with and for them.

As I drove to work the next morning, I knew the answer to the impending question: Yes, I do know what it is. It is a gift. It is life. It is healthy; it is whole. It is laughter; it is joy. It is part of me. It is my son.

Kelli S. Jones

November 15

You cannot discover new oceans unless you have the courage to lose sight of the shore.

Author Unknown

_____

_____

_____

_____

_____

_____

_____

_____

_____

_____

_____

_____

_____

_____

_____

_____

_____

November 16

Miriam looked out the big front window. Her father knelt on the ground, lifting something above his head, then driving it into the earth. A fine, gentle rain was falling, so she ran for her raincoat and boots and took her umbrella onto the porch.

"What are you doing, Daddy?" she asked.

"Planting a garden."

"We have lots of gardens," she said.

"This one is special," he said quietly. "It's for Grandma. We'll plant a mock orange bush as a memorial to her, and we'll think of Grandma whenever we see it."

He went on telling Miriam more about Grandma—her love of flowers and music, reading and cats, and how she'd say, "Mmm, smell the mock orange" every summer.

"Do you miss her?" Miriam asked.

"More than I ever thought I could. Even after I grew up, she made me feel protected."

"Who'll protect you now, Daddy?" she asked.

He raised his head. "Mommy, I guess. And Grandpa. And you," he whispered.

Miriam's mother looked out the window and saw two figures in the gloom. One digging a new garden, the other covering her father with her tiny umbrella.

Bill Petch

Just out of college, I began working at an upscale gift gallery. My morning walk to work past a small flower stand became routine. One morning I felt an overwhelming desire to buy flowers for someone. On the bottom shelf there was a nosegay of violets. Mrs. Cairns, a grey-haired widow who worked at the gallery, came to mind.

A few minutes later, I saw her standing inside the gallery doors. "These are for you, Mrs. Cairns," I said, and handed her the nosegay.

"How did you know," she said, "that today is my wedding anniversary? My husband passed away two years ago, so I'm the only one who remembers."

She took both of my hands. "My dear . . . I must tell you that I married forty years ago in a small town in Oregon. It was a cold, winter day and there were no flowers in town, so my wedding bouquet was a nosegay of violets."

Carol Fannin Rohwedder

A random act of kindness can touch
a heart in unanticipated ways.

November 18

I ended up sitting next to Julie by chance at a motivational seminar. At the end of the day, we exchanged business cards and promised to meet again soon.

When we got together for lunch, Julie casually mentioned that she'd been having random and disturbing pains in her lower legs. After endless agonizing medical tests gave her no conclusive answers, Julie began doing research of her own.

Her research pointed to Lou Gehrig's disease. She educated me about the symptoms, treatments, side effects and, worst of all, prognosis. Unfortunately, her suspicions were confirmed.

Five years after I met Julie, she was dying. We had many conversations concerning her beliefs about death and dying, how she did not want to be a burden and wanted to pass from this existence with dignity. This was a difficult yet special time for me, as I learned to honor the present moment when visiting with her.

After her death, my husband and I went to our beach cabin for the weekend. There I was able to heal and reflect on this amazingly strong and courageous woman who had taught me so much about the miracle of the human spirit.

Marlene King

November 19

 oday marks six months that my son's daddy has been deployed to Southwest Asia. But I've spent most of my life in a uniform that matches his.

We met during Desert Shield and have been through several deployments and many "TDY" trips apart from each other. We joined to serve our country and have given a combined 50 years of service to a land in which the passing flag still brings a tear to our eyes.

My husband told me last night that we would soon have to make the important decision of whether to stay in or retire for good. I tried to explain our options to our son, sure that he would say how much he missed his daddy and how much he wants him to come home.

He said, "My daddy is a great leader. He'd look good with a star."

I realized that he is the bravest, most dedicated one of all. It is he who has made the greatest sacrifice so his daddy can protect others.

Terry Hurley

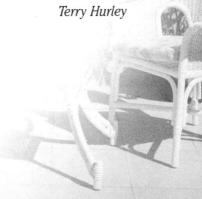

November 20

drove home from work that day wholly unprepared for what was awaiting me at home. Corey, my oldest at 21, followed me into the kitchen. He looked like a terrified little boy turning to his mommy to make things all better.

"Who's pregnant, Corey?" I asked.

He lowered his head. "Deanna."

Deanna was three months pregnant, and to compound a difficult situation, she and Corey had broken up a month earlier. He told me that as much as they yearned to be able to parent their child, they knew they were not ready, so they had decided on adoption.

They chose a couple who already had one adopted daughter. They agreed to give Corey and Deanna updates on the baby's progress.

When my grandson was born, I was filled with love and excitement one moment, sadness and loss the next. I bought a ceramic cherub for him, a guardian angel to watch over him since we wouldn't be able to.

It has been three years now, and my grandson, Tye, is doing wonderfully with his adoptive parents. I think of him every day and carry his photo in my wallet to remind me of my precious grandson and my incredible, loving son.

Debbie Rikley

I work with grieving children. One night as I was preparing to give a lecture, a woman called. She was dying and said her therapist had advised her that discussing it with her son would be too traumatic for him. I told her I thought she knew what would be best and invited her to attend the lecture.

That night I said that children usually can handle truth better than denial, and that respecting children meant including them in the family sadness, not shutting them out.

The next morning I received another phone call from the woman. When she got home from my lecture, she woke up her son and said, "Derek, I have something to tell you."

"Oh, Mommy, is it now you are going to tell me that you are dying?"

She held him close, and they both sobbed while she said, "Yes."

The little boy said he had something he had been saving for her. He handed her a dirty pencil box. Inside was a letter that said, "Good-bye, Mom. I will always love you."

The young mother died two days later. The dirty pencil box and letter were placed in her casket.

Doris Sanford

November 22

Though no one can go back and make a brand-new start, anyone can start from now and make a brand-new ending.

Anonymous

_____

_____

_____

_____

_____

_____

_____

_____

_____

_____

_____

_____

_____

_____

_____

A few months before my wedding, I spent weeknights rooting through the boxes we'd moved from the old farmhouse, deciding what was my sister's and what I should move to our new apartment. Twenty-three years of nostalgia awaited me each evening. At the bottom of one box, I discovered a homely brown clay bowl that only a child could have fashioned and only a mother could have loved. I couldn't remember making the bowl, so I assumed it was Sharon's. She denied ever seeing it, so I slipped it under her pillow.

The next morning I found it in my purse. That night, I put it in her high-school backpack. We spent the next two weeks trying to outwit each other.

A few days before the wedding, my sister approached me, towing a child's doll—about two feet high with straw-yellow hair. "Here, Gail, this is yours," she said simply. I had never seen it before, so I told her she could keep it.

On our wedding night, my husband's face turned to utter horror when I opened my suitcase. There was the yellow-haired doll atop all the clothing. My little sister really got me good.

Gail E. Strock

November 24

My firstborn has turned into a loving, well-adjusted man, I realize—marveling that he even survived his adolescence with a crumbling marriage as a backdrop and a controlling father for an antagonist. And today, we are getting ready to meet his girlfriend's parents for the first time.

Mike's step on the stairs interrupts my reverie. He plants a kiss on my cheek and presents me with an unwrapped box filled with travel brochures for the Hawaiian Islands. I almost made it to the islands three years ago, but my mother became ill and I had to cancel my flight.

"I can't wait to read these at my leisure."

"Have a look now," he insists.

I work through the brochures and find an envelope at the bottom of the stack. I gasp as I open the envelope to find a gift certificate for an open-ended, prepaid, round-trip airline ticket to Oahu.

"I can't accept this from you." My voice crept to a whisper. "You work too hard for your money."

"Mom, who deserves it more than you?"

Barbara Feder Mendel

November 25

I went out to dinner with my mother and my daughters. Kevin, my husband, was working in Charleston. We had a nice evening. My daughters and I had just arrived in Waterloo the night before, so my mom and I spent the meal catching up. She asked me about Kevin's deployment and how he liked his new squadron.

When it came time to pay the bill, the waitress told us it had already been taken care of by a man sitting near us. Our benefactor was embarrassed since he had intended for his gesture to be anonymous.

He looked at me and said, "I overheard you say that your husband was in the military. Thank you for all that you do, and please thank your husband for defending our country."

Jennifer Minor

November 26

The Depression took a toll on my parents' relationship, and when I was 18, they divorced. Daddy never had a close relationship with his six children and drifted farther away after the divorce.

Several years later he married a wonderful woman who had two sons. Under her influence we became a "blended family." She always treated us as if we were her own children.

At the time of our father's death, we asked our other mother if my mother (Daddy's first wife) could attend his funeral.

Without giving it a second thought, she immediately replied, "Of course, honey—she's the mother of my children."

Jewel Sanders

hanksgiving Day had arrived in New England. My 12-year-old twins and I had recently moved to a Boston suburb while adjusting to a painful divorce. We had been invited to spend the holiday with a deacon's family from our church.

We enjoyed the day along with another guest named Tinker, who was unusually quiet. Our host excused himself after pumpkin pie to give Tinker a ride home. Soon after, we left, too.

As Christmas drew near, I wondered how I would buy the gifts the children wanted and a tree and food for dinner.

A friend helped us cut a small, spindly Christmas tree. I had saved a chicken in the freezer for dinner.

Four days later, I pulled a bundle of letters from the mailbox. A small envelope with no return address caught my eye. In it was a card and four hundred-dollar bills.

The children grew up and left home. I remarried. When we attended my son's graduation, we visited the deacon who had welcomed us that Thanksgiving. I told the story of the anonymous blessing. He said, "That young man, Tinker, was a convicted murderer serving a life sentence. He asked me to come by the prison and pick up some money for you and the children. He gave you all he had."

Judith Gillis

**Human kindness and compassion
can work through anyone.**

November 28

Start by doing what's necessary,
then what's possible, and suddenly
you are doing the impossible.

St. Francis of Assisi

_____

_____

_____

_____

_____

_____

_____

_____

_____

_____

_____

_____

_____

_____

November 29

*M*y family was separated and placed into foster care when I was five years old. We grew up in separate homes, never knowing each other. The only memory that remained of my family was of a tall, slender woman always being there to comfort me.

On my forty-fifth birthday, a card arrived in the mail with a return name and address of someone I didn't recognize. The short note read, "I was thinking of you on your birthday. Mom."

For two weeks the card lay on the table, tearing at my heart. Finally, summoning up my courage, I got her number and dialed. Just as I was about to hang up, a voice from the past said, "Hello." It was my older sister. Mom had died two weeks after sending the card.

As we talked, reacquainting ourselves, I asked what my mom looked like. My sister told me she was a very short, stocky lady. Then who was the tall, slender woman that I remembered?

Our life began returning to me. For two years my older sister was the one caring for us. "By the way," I asked before hanging up, "how tall are you?"

She answered, "Five-foot-nine."

Nora Steuber-Tamblin

November 30

A year after my mother died, I faced my first Christmas without her, and my sadness dampened the day's usual excitement. I was supposed to be at my best friend Rebecca's house for dinner, but I chose not to leave the shelter of my small apartment. My eyes were red and sore from the tears that would not stop.

I must have drifted off to sleep, for I awakened when someone pounded at the front door. I looked through the window and saw Rebecca's car parked out front.

"Girlfriend!" she shouted. "I know you're in there."

"Leave me alone!" I shouted back.

I heard paper rustling as she slid something under the door. When I was sure she had left, I retrieved the small square package. It contained a gold pen, a journal and a bookmark with a note on it:

Dear Sister Friend,

My words won't heal the pain. But your own words can.
Love,
Rebecca

Over the following months, my emotions took refuge within the pages of the book. As I healed, I understood the incredible friendship Rebecca and I shared. When I pushed her away, she found a way to help me communicate my grief.

S. A. (Shae) Cooke

id taught the staff and patients alike that there's room for life and laughter in a hospice. He was a born actor with a wonderful sense of theater. Often he played to the gallery, which in this case was the three other patients who shared the same room.

One morning, I was giving out the medication when he hoisted himself onto his elbows, looked across the room and muttered, "What day is it today?"

I answered, "Palm Sunday."

"Then today is a good day to die," and he fell back on the bed. A few seconds later, he popped open his eyes, looked at me and sighed.

Later that same week, he decided to give a repeat performance. "What day is it today?" he asked.

"It's Good Friday."

Without looking up from his book, his roommate muttered loudly, "I hope to God he doesn't die today—he might rise again on Sunday!"

Dennis Sibley as told to Allen Klein

**Look for humor in a sad situation,
and you will find it.**

December 2

There are four skills that any true traveler must master: patience, tolerance, respect and a sense of humor.

I was in Bhubaneshwar, in the eastern state of Orissa, India, and had just spent the afternoon scrambling around the ruins of a thirteenth-century Surya temple. It was hot and dusty. All I wanted was a sealed, safe bottle of cold water.

We pulled up to the hotel grounds, and I went to the desk and asked for a bottle of water.

"Please to go to your room, Ma'am. It will be delivered."

Knowing that the kitchen was just behind the desk, I pleaded with the man.

"Yes, Ma'am, it will be delivered shortly," he responded with a smile.

Exasperated, I slumped off to my room and stewed until there was a knock at my door.

And there before me stood three men balancing a refrigerator, inside of which was one bottle of ice-cold water.

Lucy Izon

Nobody trips over mountains.
It is the small pebble that causes you to
stumble. Pass all the pebbles in your path,
and you will find you have
crossed the mountain.

Source Unknown

_____

_____

_____

_____

_____

_____

_____

_____

_____

_____

_____

_____

_____

_____

December 4

At the end of her shift, Lois, a surgical and intensive care nurse for 30 years, was eager to go home to a hot bath and a novel. Instead, she wound up climbing into an ambulance and accompanying the paramedics to the scene of a two-car accident.

Lois attended to the woman in one of the vehicles. Hoping to comfort the woman, she said, "Looks like you're gong to be fine, but just to be on the safe side, we'll take you in." Mutely, the woman stared at Lois with vacant eyes. En route to the hospital, Lois held the patient's hands and comforted her.

The following morning Lois checked on the accident victim. The patient blinked her eyes. "Are you real, or are you an angel?"

Lois smiled. "Nurses are often referred to as angels of mercy."

The woman shook her head. "Last night, I was in an accident and thought I might die. An angel appeared, and when she touched me, I felt a surge of love and knew she had been sent to reassure me that I would live. You look and sound exactly like her, except you don't have wings."

Sally Kelly-Engeman

*F*or months, we looked forward to the new baby sister. When the day finally arrived, my husband rushed me to the hospital, while my in-laws got the boys ready to go meet their little sister.

With a piercing scream, Becky came into the world and was just as beautiful as we had imagined. My husband rushed out the delivery-room door to get the boys while the nurse pushed Becky and me into the hallway.

"Brad and Chad, this is Becky," Roy proudly announced.

I noticed Chad wiping tears from his eyes and looking all around.

"What's wrong, Chad?" I asked.

"Where's my little sister? Becky is Brad's sister; Candy was supposed to be mine."

As my in-laws left to take the boys home, Chad continued to look around for his missing baby.

For several months their bedtime prayers ended with: "Thank you for our little sister. Please give us another."

Becky was a colicky baby. After about three months of sleepless nights, I heard the boys change their prayer slightly. "Thank you for our little sister, but we don't need another one."

Nancy B. Gibbs

December 6

As a child I spent hours in my small backyard playhouse, complete with a mailbox made from a coffee can. One summer day I asked my mother if she could bring me some mail.

I busied myself until I heard her high voice call out, "Mail time." Inside a tiny box were two sticks of Juicy Fruit gum; a square of waxed paper wrapped around a handful of chocolate chips, raisins and miniature marshmallows; and a new Pink Pearl eraser. There was a seed catalog, as well as three envelopes addressed to "Patty, Playhouse, Back Yard, Oregon" and posted with an S&H Green Stamp. In one was a page of notepaper.

How are you doing? It's been beautiful weather here, though a little hot for me. I've been canning beans. We have a lovely, large garden, as usual. Do come visit us. You know you are always welcome.
Love, Mama.

Forty years later, remembering the mailbox, I realized that the mother who took time from her work to gather up some junk mail and trinkets to put into a package, write a personal note and deliver it, all in true play-acting style, was my special companion, even back then.

Patty Duncan

December 7

Though she had been in a coma for nearly six months, it was still a shock when my grandmother passed away. There would a typical Catholic send-off with four wakes and a funeral.

The awkwardness at the funeral home came to an end with the arrival of my friend Kelly. We had been friends since she was three and I four.

Kelly came right to me. In her hands were two packages of M&Ms, original and peanut. "I thought this would make you feel better," she said. For the rest of the wake and the others that Kelly attended, we sat in the back of the viewing room, eating M&Ms and talking quietly. A devastating and unfamiliar experience had suddenly become easier to bear, with a childhood offering of chocolate candies and the company of a devoted friend.

Jennifer Stevens

December 8

One of our favorite patients had been in and out of our small, rural hospital several times. We had all grown quite attached to her and her husband.

I admired their expression of love. Daily he brought her fresh flowers and a smile, then sat by her bed as they held hands and talked quietly. Every night before he left, he closed the door so they could spend time alone together.

On this night, however, things were different. She had taken a turn for the worse and wouldn't make it through the night. I checked in on her first, asked if they needed anything, then left quickly. I offered comfort throughout the evening, and at about midnight she passed away.

"May I please be alone with her for awhile?" he asked, and I closed the door behind me.

Suddenly, the most beautiful male voice floated from that room singing "Beautiful Brown Eyes" at the top of his lungs. When the tune faded, he called to me. "I sang that song to her every night from the first day we met. Tonight I had to make sure she heard me as she was on her way to heaven."

Christy M. Martin

Express love daily, all the way to the end.

My son has been deaf since birth. He was 14 when we were told he was losing his eyesight and would eventually be completely blind.

I asked Kevin, "Before things really change, what one thing do you want to see more than anything else?"

He thought for a while and then said, "A volcano . . . I want to see a volcano in Hawaii."

I contacted an organization that fulfills the wishes of chronically and critically ill children, and within a couple of weeks we were on a plane bound for Honolulu.

On the morning of the big day, we climbed into a helicopter and headed toward the volcano. As we hovered over the cinder cone, Kevin dropped his offering for Pele, the fire goddess, as a symbol of good luck. Then he signed, "I wish she can be strong for an eruption."

As we watched, a tiny eruption began before our very eyes—Pele's gift to Kevin.

April MacNeil

December 10

Dorothy was a mother of four young children who desperately needed the court-ordered child support from her ex-husband, already a year in arrears. Though she knew it would do no good, Dorothy went to the district attorney and swore out a complaint against her ex-husband. "That way, if he ever does get any money, I will get it," she told a friend.

But Dorothy neither received money nor even satisfaction.

One morning she awoke with a strange sense that she should close out the complaint. *He isn't paying now*, her inner voice said. *You are.* Because the thought persisted, she did cancel the complaint. She felt sudden relief, as if a heavy burden had been lifted. The next day Dorothy's boss called her into the office and gave her an unexpected promotion. The net increase in salary was $100 a month more than the court-ordered child support.

Bobbie Reed

To be free, let go of the desire for revenge.

*When one door of happiness closes,
another door opens; but often
we look so long at the closed door
that we do not see the one
which has opened for us.*

Helen Keller

_____

_____

_____

_____

_____

_____

_____

_____

_____

_____

_____

_____

_____

December 12

It was after the hotel call, the one where a desk clerk found "no one registered under that name," that I called my husband's office hoping for a hotel mix-up. A few months later, my husband filed for divorce.

Several years later, I was thinking about how much pain I could have avoided. I sat down with a notepad and pen and began spilling out words of healing, a few lines at a time. When I ran out of thoughts, I stuck the pages in a desk drawer.

I took them out later and realized they read like greeting-card verses, but I had no funds to hire an artist. I put the notes back in the drawer.

Then it occurred to me that I did know one artist. I called my former husband. After hearing a few of the verses, he said he'd love to design original art and would provide the money for the printing costs as well.

I named the cards "Ex's & Oh's."

My cards have been sent to spouses, children, parents, in-laws and friends going through a divorce. As one woman said, "Thank you for being a light in the darkness."

Jan Nations

An idea that keeps presenting itself will one day turn into reality.

My sister Cynthia began volunteering at a local hospital the summer she was 16. Occasionally I would stop by and walk her home.

One day I found her in the room of a young boy whose eyes were heavily bandaged. I heard my sister describing what she saw from his window—the blue sky, the garden with clusters of flowers and leafy green shrubs.

Suddenly, she moved to the window and said with excitement, "A little brown and white spotted terrier just jumped into the garden. Now he's running around in circles, stopping to dig holes. He's having such fun, David."

I heard the boy laugh out loud, and his face lit up with excitement underneath the bandage.

"Oh, oh," Cynthia said, "looks like the fun is over. One of the staff just came out and chased him off."

I waited patiently for my sister at the nurse's station. She arrived soon after, happy as always. When I joined that boy in seeing the world through my sister's eyes, I found myself looking into her heart.

Robert C. Fuentes

The human heart is seen
through the people it influences.

December 14

Call it any old psychobabble thing you want, whatever it was, the fact remained that I was not my usual cheerful self from the end of January until mid-March.

One day after a job interview, I stopped at my friend Sharon's house for tea. As I was leaving, Sharon noticed I was missing a button on the belt of my coat. "Hey," she said, "there's an extra button inside. I'll sew it on for you right now."

The gift of Sharon's time, when I was at such a low state, meant more to me than if someone had given me a sweepstakes check.

When I got home there was a silly greeting card from another friend. "I've got a hug here with your name on it."

A few days later, my Texas coauthor sent me a "sunshine box" filled with chocolates, red silk tulips and ginger-lily bath gel.

Before I knew it, I understood one of the most amazing, most profound aspects of life: The world and its people are designed in such a way that no matter how big our problems, the smallest gesture given in love from a friend can become the biggest miracle of all.

Patricia Lorenz

The day I had to stop dead in my tracks in the aisle of a busy supermarket was one of the worst in my life. I was pregnant, and so large I had long since forgotten what either my feet or my legs looked like. During one of the hottest Augusts on record, going anywhere was torture. But we were out of milk.

In all my magazines, the maternity advertisements showed blissful mothers-to-be in adorable outfits, perfect hairdos—even high heels. Here I was: miserable, a whole month past my due date, with cramps in both feet so excruciating I couldn't move. My face beet-red, I pretended not to notice the angry shoppers whose way I was blocking, and then I heard a little girl's voice: "Mommy, why does that lady look so funny?"

That mother said something that was a blessing to me during those final miserable days and during my next two pregnancies as well: "It's because God has given that woman a tiny baby to carry next to her heart."

And even after our children are born, we mothers will carry them next to our hearts our whole lives long.

Bonnie Compton Hanson

December 16

When my friend, Sadie, was taken to the emergency room, I rushed over to be with her as soon as I received the news.

Sadie was both surprised and pleased to see me. "How did you get them to let you in?" she asked.

I knew Sadie needed a friend to comfort her, so on the drive over I had decided that if worse came to worst, I would be forced to tell a lie and say I was Sadie's sister.

After I explained all this to Sadie, she threw back her head in hearty laughter. While I was trying to figure out why she was laughing, I glanced down at our clasped hands—my very white one held gently between her two black ones.

June Cerza Kolf

Friends are sisters under the skin.

December 17

*I*n the picture that my ex-husband's girlfriend ripped in half, I am wearing a white blouse and yellow gathered skirt. I am sitting on the edge of a fountain in Paris, and I'm laughing because I've had a summer of freedom, I'm 17, and I'm in love with the boy taking the picture. And we're in Paris.

The boy and I walked for miles, climbed the Eiffel Tower and tossed coins in every fountain we saw. With the last of my money I bought a miniscule bottle of perfume, L'Air du Temps, and made it last for months.

Many years have gone by. The boy and I got married, and after 19 years and four daughters, we ended up in a bitter divorce. But the girl in the snapshot is dazzled by a future that shimmers as bright as the fountain behind her. All the tears and pain destined to divide us lie ahead— and I wouldn't change a thing.

Because once in a while, I catch the scent of L'Air du Temps, and I'm in Paris again, and 17.

Marilyn McFarlane

*Knowing all the tears and pain
that lie ahead, you wouldn't change a thing.*

December 18

My 24-year friendship with Vickie was cemented by a history of combined convictions, confidences and confessions. State lines had separated us. Crowded schedules had fragmented us. But we never let that interfere. Instead, we nourished our relationship long-distance.

As I continued the bedside vigil of our 23-year-old who lay comatose, wasting away in a Los Angeles trauma unit, there was only one person I wanted and needed: my friend Vickie. She would be helpful and hopeful. I needed both.

Suddenly, I felt a deep kinship with the pioneer I once read about who found herself, at the end of her trek, on the Great Plains—pregnant, heartsick and isolated.

Alone.

My pleas joined hers as she cried into her diary, "I don't want a doctor. I want a woman."

Carol McAdoo Rehme

December 19

*The secret of happiness is not
in doing what one likes to do,
but liking what one has to do.*

J. M. Barrie

December 20

His brief but tormented young life was punctuated by recurring visits to hospital emergency rooms for treatment of unexplained, questionable injuries too numerous to count. The family, friends and social system that were intended to protect this young lad failed him miserably.

On his last hospital admission, this battered and wounded youngster received exceptional care. The nurse who was taking care of this broken four-year-old climbed into his bed, lay down next to him and cuddled him close to her heart. She stroked his forehead and sang soft lullabies in his ear until he fell asleep. That night he closed his eyes for the last time, and those beautiful lullabies were the last sounds he would ever hear.

Laura Hayes Lagana

December 21

As I approached a half a century young, I was given the best surprise of my life—a weekend at the Calistoga Hot Springs with my best friend, my sister, Arlie P.

After a fabulous meal we checked into our room at the spa. We came alive with conversation and strolled down Main Street, disappearing into dress shops and gift shops as we talked.

We sat in hot tubs and then in the steam spa. Once we'd had enough heat, I spent 15 minutes of total relaxation with cucumbers on my eyelids. I nearly fell asleep.

The treatment ended with a full-body massage.

By Sunday morning I realized that hot oils, mud baths, steam saunas, lotions and wraps can rejuvenate wrinkled, tired skin. For a bit. A day. A week. But a strong bond between sisters lasts forever, keeping one's soul rejuvenated for eternity.

Janie Emaus

December 22

When you pack your bags to explore the beauties of your own country or to travel around the world, consider these keys to a happy journey:

Travel lightly. You are not traveling for people to see you!

Travel slowly.

Travel expectantly. Every place is like a surprise package.

Travel hopefully.

Travel humbly. Respect traditions and ways of life.

Travel courteously.

Travel gratefully.

Travel with an open mind.

Travel with curiosity.

Travel with imagination.

Travel fearlessly.

Travel relaxed.

Travel patiently. It takes time to understand others.

Travel with the spirit of a world citizen. You'll discover that people are basically much the same the world around. Be an ambassador of goodwill to all people.

Wilferd A. Peterson, submitted by Rebecca Esparza

We are all travelers through the journey of life.

December 23

*If a child is to keep alive his inborn sense
of wonder, he needs the companionship
of at least one adult who can share it,
rediscovering with him the joy,
excitement and mystery of the world we live in.*

Source Unknown

_____

_____

_____

_____

_____

_____

_____

_____

_____

_____

_____

_____

_____

_____

December 24

Alice's mother died when she was five years old. The year was 1925, and life was hard. Alice, who grew up to be my mother, told me that her family was too poor to even afford to give her a doll.

In December 1982, I worked at a local bank. One of my customers approached me with a sample of her handiwork: beautiful, handmade dolls. She was taking orders for Christmas. I decided to get one for my five-year-old daughter and then asked my customer if she could make me a special doll for my mother—one with gray hair and spectacles: a grandmother doll.

Christmas Day arrived, and so did Santa Claus. As he turned to leave he retrieved one more gift from his knapsack. The card read:

For Alice:

I was cleaning out my sleigh before my trip this year and came across this package that was supposed to be delivered on December 25, 1925. The present inside has aged, but I felt that you might still wish to have it. Many apologies for the lateness of the gift.

Love,
Santa Claus

That doll, given by "Santa," 57 years late, made my mother the happiest "child" alive.

Alice Ferguson

December 25

The year I was seven, my mother, three brothers and I made the long drive home from Grandma's house. Leaving us safely sleeping in the car, my mother entered our house. As soon as she opened the door, she realized we had been robbed. They had taken our tree, the presents, even the stockings.

Carrying us in one by one, my mother put us to bed. It was two in the morning, but her children were still going to have a Christmas. She would see to that.

Early Christmas morning, we hurried to the living room and stopped in the doorway, confused by the strange magic that had turned our beautiful Christmas spruce into a small, bare, pear-shaped tree leaning against the wall. My mother told us that someone really poor had needed our tree and stockings, but we were very lucky because we had one another.

After breakfast we made ornaments out of old egg cartons and cereal boxes. We laughed, sang carols and decorated our new tree.

Although I do not remember what I got on other Christmases, I have never forgotten the year someone stole our Christmas and gave us the unexpected gift of joyous togetherness and love.

Christina Chanes Nystrom

December 26

On our way to a ski vacation, our Jeep hit black ice and rolled over. Miraculously, all of us survived the accident. The only serious injury any of us sustained was a shattered left arm—mine.

With lots of titanium in my arm and still taking an enormous amount of painkillers, I arrived at the apartment I shared with Stacey, a woman whom I barely knew.

As I learned later, Stacey sat down with David, my doctor friend who drove me home from the hospital, and questioned him about my state and my needs. She called all my girlfriends whose numbers I could find, got David to have our mutual friends call her, and within a few days, she had a very efficient operation going.

Stacey took most morning and evening shifts, did my shopping and laundry, and gave me a sponge bath every other day. I spent most of my time with Stacey.

Fully recovered now, my life is completely different. My injury took a lot out of me, but it also made me reassess my priorities and gave me a great friend who has become a cornerstone of my new life.

Monika Szamko

The Bangkok airport was stifling, and I was exhausted. All I wanted to do was make my flight to Chiang Mai.

I strapped myself into my seat and saw a little boy walking hand in hand with the flight attendant toward the plane. She asked if he could sit next to me.

When the engines started to roar, I knew he was scared. I noticed he had brought a pad of paper with him, and I thought if I gave him my pen he could draw pictures to keep himself busy. He gingerly took the pen and thanked me in Thai.

I was absorbed in my materials when I felt a gentle touch on my hand. He had drawn an enchanting picture of flowers, animals and trees on the pad. We both smiled.

At snack time, we shared what we had, then I went back to my reading, and he started drawing again. Another gentle tap. To my amazement, he had drawn a perfect picture of my face.

The plane set down, and the attendant came and got the boy. I waved and held up my picture as he got off the plane and ran to meet his parents.

Nancy Mills

December 28

I long to accomplish great and noble tasks,
but it is my chief duty to accomplish
small tasks as if they were great and noble.

Helen Keller

_____

_____

_____

_____

_____

_____

_____

_____

_____

_____

_____

_____

_____

*O*ne day, a very troubled little girl came through the door of my day nursery. She was born in prison after her mom had used marijuana, crack and cocaine her entire pregnancy. I knew her progress would be a mighty battle.

As months rolled on, I began to bond with this child who no one wanted. Daily, we sat in the big rocking chair in my office. I sang "Jesus Loves Me," and she always settled down and became very still. Though she never spoke, peace seemed to fill her face as she listened.

One day after a very long battle, I held her to again calm her fears and pain. In silence we rocked back and forth. Then she spoke a complete sentence for the first time, "Sing to me about that Man who loves me."

Alicia Hill

December 30

*A*ge hasn't taken the explorer out of Aunt Anne. Her husband died, leaving her alone at their home in New York's Catskill Mountains. She woke up one day and proclaimed, "Well, if life's going to blow some wind into my sails, I better get my boat out."

She shoved off in a little mobile home in Florida. Her only baggage was the overflow of her creative spirit: clay for sculpting, music, poetry. At age 75, she faced an adventure she thought she would never enjoy again: love.

She and Jack had been married for seven years when she suggested they take a vacation in the Catskills. As they explored the woods, Jack let go of Aunt Anne's hand and fell to the ground. He passed away before the ambulance reached the hospital.

I fretted for her and wondered how she would handle this turn of events. But she moved to Wisconsin to be near her son and grandchildren. I received word from her not long ago. "I'm so excited about the sculpting classes I'm teaching in Madison. Isn't it wonderful?" *Yes, it is,* I thought. Aunt Anne was still in the thick of it.

Anne Marion as told to Eileen Lawrence

When life blows wind into your sails, you had better get your boat out.

*S*ix months ago, I had moved from the lush southeast coast to a desolate part of west Texas to live with my mom while I recuperated from a serious accident. New Year's Eve was only a week away, and I didn't have even the prospect of a date. Was the rest of the year going to be like this?

Usually the prospect of a blind date would have made me shudder, but I was determined not to spend the night watching other people enjoy themselves, so I called a coworker.

She had been asked out by someone who didn't know she was engaged, and he had asked if she had a friend. Nervously, I accepted.

My date turned out to be a cowboy! Over dinner we never ran out of things to talk about, and I couldn't take my eyes off those green eyes and that smiling mouth.

The next morning, early, he called. Fifty-six days later we were married. That was 21 years ago, and even after all that time, his kisses still make me lightheaded.

Judith L. Robinson

Don't just watch other people enjoy life.
Ask life to give you what you want.

Permissions

January 1, adapted from "Bowled Over," originally published in *Chicken Soup for the Single's Soul* ©1999.

January 2, adapted from "New Job," originally published in *Chicken Soup for the Nurse's Soul* ©2001.

January 3, adapted from "Confessions of a Stepmother," originally published in *Chicken Soup for the Mother's Soul 2* ©2001.

January 4, adapted from "My Sisters, Myself and the Seasons of Life," originally published in *Chicken Soup for the Sister's Soul* ©2002.

January 5, adapted from "With a Little Help from a Stranger," originally published in *Life Lessons for Women* ©2004.

January 6, adapted from "Anna," originally published in *Chicken Soup for the Teacher's Soul* ©2002.

January 7, originally published in *Chicken Soup for the Traveler's Soul* ©2002.

January 8, adapted from "Beautiful Day, Isn't It?" originally published in *Chicken Soup for the Golden Soul* ©2000.

January 9, adapted from "An Educated Woman," originally published in *Chicken Soup for the Single's Soul* ©1999.

January 10, adapted from "The Problem Class," originally published in *Chicken Soup for the Teacher's Soul* ©2002.

January 11, originally published in *Chicken Soup for the Traveler's Soul* ©2002.

January 12, adapted from "Revenge of the Fifth-Grade Girls," originally published in *Chicken Soup for the Sister's Soul* ©2002.

January 13, adapted from "On Being the Mother of Twins," originally published in *Chicken Soup for the Expectant Mother's Soul* ©2000.

January 14, adapted from "We Chose to Be Friends," originally published in *Chicken Soup for the Sister's Soul* ©2002.

January 15, adapted from "Woman's Best Friend," originally published in *Chicken Soup for the Cat and Dog Lover's Soul* ©1999.

January 16, adapted from "Gramma Jan," originally published in *Chicken Soup for the Grandparent's Soul* ©2002.

January 17, adapted from "Help for the Helper," originally published in *Chicken Soup for the Golden Soul* ©2000.

January 18, adapted from "Silky's Test," originally published in *Chicken Soup for the Cat and Dog Lover's Soul* ©1999.

January 19, adapted from "My Life: The Sitcom," originally published in *Chicken Soup for the Sister's Soul* ©2002.

January 20, adapted from "Behind the Mirror," originally published in *Chicken Soup for the Grandparent's Soul* ©2002.

January 21, adapted from "Stranded on an Island," originally published in *Chicken Soup for the Mother's Soul 2* ©2001.

January 22, adapted from "Love Is Just Like a Broken Arm," originally published in *Chicken Soup for the Single's Soul* ©1999.

January 23, adapted from "One Finger," originally published in *Chicken Soup for the Grandparent's Soul* ©2002.

January 24, adapted from "Encouraging Kelly," originally published in *Chicken Soup for the Teacher's Soul* ©2002.

January 25, originally published in *Chicken Soup for the Cat and Dog Lover's Soul* ©1999.

January 26, adapted from "In the Eye of the Storm," originally published in *Chicken Soup for the Golden Soul* ©2000.

January 27, adapted from "The Importance of Conscience," originally published in *Chicken Soup for the Sister's Soul* ©2002.

January 28, adapted from "A Dream Deferred," originally published in *Chicken Soup for the Golden Soul* ©2000.

January 29, adapted from "The Therapy Team," originally published in *Chicken Soup for the Cat and Dog Lover's Soul* ©1999.

January 30, adapted from "Can You Love Me?" originally published in *Chicken Soup for the Single's Soul* ©1999.

January 31, adapted from "A Random Harvest," originally published in *Chicken Soup for the Teacher's Soul* ©2002.

February 1, originally published in *Chicken Soup for the Military Wife's Soul* ©2005.

February 2, adapted from "Sergei," originally published in *Chicken Soup for the Teacher's Soul* ©2002.

February 3, adapted from "A Timeless Tapestry," originally published in *Chicken Soup for the Golden Soul* ©2000.

February 4, adapted from "Chicken Pox Diary," originally published in *Chicken Soup for the Mother's Soul 2* ©2001.

February 5, adapted from "Santa Redeemed," originally published in *Chicken Soup for the Single's Soul* ©1999.

February 6, adapted from "Same Agenda," originally published in *Chicken Soup for the Grandparent's Soul* ©2002.

February 7, adapted from "It's Never Too Late," excerpted from *Chocolate for a Woman's Soul* by Kay Allenbaugh, originally published in *Chicken Soup for the Golden Soul* ©2000.

February 8, adapted from "Grandma and the Chicken Pox," originally published in *Chicken Soup for the Grandparent's Soul* ©2002.

February 9, adapted from "A Promise to Roxanne," as appeared in *Woman's World,* originally published in *Chicken Soup for the Sister's Soul* ©2002.

February 10, adapted from "Enjoying the Moment," originally published in *Life Lessons for Women* ©2004.

February 11, adapted from "The Cat Who Needed a Night Light," originally published in *Chicken Soup for the Cat and Dog Lover's Soul* ©1999.

February 12, adapted from "The Miracle of My Sister's Laughing," originally published in *Chicken Soup for the Sister's Soul* ©2002.

February 13, adapted from "Benjamin," originally published in *Chicken Soup for the Teacher's Soul* ©2002.

February 14, originally published in *Chicken Soup for the Military Wife's Soul* ©2005.

February 15, adapted from "Eric," originally published in *Chicken Soup for the Teacher's Soul* ©2002.

February 16, adapted from "A Cat Named Turtle," originally published in *Chicken Soup for the Cat and Dog Lover's Soul* ©1999.

February 17, adapted from "The Diary," originally published in *Chicken Soup for the Sister's Soul* ©2002.

February 18, adapted from "Five Dates, Eleven Hundred Letters and Fifty-Five Years Later," originally published in *Chicken Soup for the Golden Soul* ©2000.

February 19, adapted from "Remembering to Forget," originally published in *Chicken Soup for the Golden Soul* ©2000.

February 20, adapted from "Lightning's Gift," originally published in *Chicken Soup for the Single's Soul* ©1999.

February 21, originally published in *Chicken Soup for the Military Wife's Soul* ©2005.

February 22, adapted from "Sunglasses," originally published in *Chicken Soup for the Mother's Soul 2* ©2001.

February 23, adapted from "Where Do Babies Come From?" originally published in *Chicken Soup for the Nurse's Soul* ©2001.

February 24, adapted from "Computer Granny," originally published in *Chicken Soup for the Grandparent's Soul* ©2002.

February 25, adapted from "Hands to Go 'Round," originally published in *Chicken Soup for the Single's Soul* ©1999.

February 26, adapted from "The Age of Mystique," excerpted from *Chocolate for a Woman's Soul* by Kay Allenbaugh, originally published in *Chicken Soup for the Golden Soul* ©2000.

February 27, adapted from "Comfort Zones," originally published in *Chicken Soup for the Sister's Soul* ©2002.

February 28, adapted from "The Princess and the Toad," originally published in *Chicken Soup for the Cat and Dog Lover's Soul* ©1999.

March 1, adapted from "All Things Grow . . . with Love," originally published in *Chicken Soup for the Teacher's Soul* ©2002.

March 2, adapted from "Have Freedom, Will Travel," originally published in *Chicken Soup for the Single's Soul* ©1999.

March 3, adapted from "Cultivating My Garden," originally published in *Chicken Soup for the Single's Soul* ©1999.

March 4, originally published in *Chicken Soup for the Military Wife's Soul* ©2005.

March 5, adapted from "Unk's Fiddle," originally published in *Chicken Soup for the Single's Soul* ©1999.

March 6, adapted from "We'll Never Divorce You," originally published in *Chicken Soup for the Grandparent's Soul* ©2002.

March 7, adapted from "Communication Is the Key," originally published in *Chicken Soup for the Nurse's Soul* ©2001.

March 8, adapted from "Happy Anniversary," originally published in *Chicken Soup for the Golden Soul* ©2000.

March 9, adapted from "The Green Pajamas," originally published in *Chicken Soup for the Mother's Soul 2* ©2001.

March 10, adapted from "Begin at the Beginning," originally published in *Chicken Soup for the Teacher's Soul* ©2002.

March 11, adapted from "Roses in December," originally published in *Chicken Soup for the Teacher's Soul* ©2002.

March 12, adapted from "Are You Sure?" originally published in *Chicken Soup for the Sister's Soul* ©2002.

March 13, adapted from "Making the Rest the Best," originally published in *Chicken Soup for the Golden Soul* ©2000.

March 14, adapted from "Me and My Mewse," originally published in *Chicken Soup for the Cat and Dog Lover's Soul* ©1999.

March 15, originally published in *Chicken Soup for the Military Wife's Soul* ©2005.

March 16, adapted from "Banana, Anyone?" originally published in *Chicken Soup for the Golden Soul* ©2000.

March 17, adapted from "Circle of Love," originally published in *Chicken Soup for the Cat and Dog Lover's Soul* ©1999.

March 18, adapted from "The Intruder," originally published in *Chicken Soup for the Sister's Soul* ©2002.

March 19, adapted from "Pumpkin Magic," originally published in *Chicken Soup for the Grandparent's Soul* ©2002.

March 20, originally published in *Chicken Soup for the Military Wife's Soul* ©2005.

March 21, adapted from "Parking in the Center of the Garage," originally published in *Life Lessons for Women* ©2004.

March 22, adapted from "Pony," originally published in *Chicken Soup for the Nurse's Soul* ©2001.

March 23, adapted from "Feeling Free," originally published in *Life Lessons for Women* ©2004.

March 24, adapted from "My Previous Life," originally published in *Chicken Soup for the Expectant Mother's Soul* ©2000.

March 25, adapted from "Grammy's Gifts," originally published in *Chicken Soup for the Grandparent's Soul* ©2002.

March 26, adapted from "It Just Isn't Fair," originally published in *Chicken Soup for the Mother's Soul* ©1997.

March 27, adapted from "Baby Toys," originally published in *Chicken Soup for the Expectant Mother's Soul* ©2000.

March 28, adapted from "The Grandma Video," originally published in *Chicken Soup for the Grandparent's Soul* ©2002.

March 29, adapted from "Baby Mall," originally published in *Chicken Soup for the Expectant Mother's Soul* © 2000.

March 30, adapted from "Turning the Page," originally published in *Chicken Soup for the Single's Soul* ©1999.

March 31, adapted from "A Letter to My Preschoolers," originally published in *Chicken Soup for the Teacher's Soul* ©2002.

April 1, adapted from "Dancing in the Street," originally published in *Chicken Soup for the Parent's Soul* ©2000.

April 2, adapted from "So He Must Be Right, Huh?" originally published in *Chicken Soup for the Writer's Soul* ©2000.

April 3, originally published in *Chicken Soup for the Traveler's Soul* ©2002.

April 4, adapted from "A Cruise and a Promise," originally published in *Chicken Soup for the Traveler's Soul* ©2002.

April 5, adapted from "Knowing What Your Rope Is," originally published in *Life Lessons for Women* ©2004.

April 6, adapted from "A Visit with My Parents," originally published in *Chicken Soup for the Traveler's Soul* ©2002.

April 7, adapted from "Marriage and Metaphors: A Writer's Life on and off the Pages," originally published in *Chicken Soup for the Writer's Soul* ©2000.

April 8, adapted from "The Photograph Album," originally published in *Chicken Soup for the Parent's Soul* ©2000.

April 9, adapted from "Forgiveness," originally published in *Chicken Soup for the Parent's Soul* ©2000.

April 10, adapted from "The Secret Handshake," originally published in *Chicken Soup for the Mother's Soul 2* ©2001.

April 11, adapted from "Seven Days and Seventy Miles," originally published in *Chicken Soup for the Traveler's Soul* ©2002.

April 12, originally published in *Chicken Soup for the Traveler's Soul* ©2002.

April 13, adapted from "Why I Keep Writing," originally published in *Chicken Soup for the Writer's Soul* ©2000.

April 14, adapted from "Earning My Wings," originally published in *Chicken Soup for the Traveler's Soul* ©2002.

April 15, adapted from "A Sweet Lesson," originally published in *Chicken Soup for the Mother's Soul 2* ©2001.

April 16, adapted from "Bosom Buddies," originally published in *Chicken Soup for the Girlfriend's Soul* ©2004.

April 17, adapted from "Legacy," originally published in *Chicken Soup for the Writer's Soul* ©2000.

April 18, originally published in *Chicken Soup for the Parent's Soul* ©2000.

April 19, adapted from "Prayer Flags," originally published in *Chicken Soup for the Soul of America* ©2002.

April 20, adapted from "The Real Hero," originally published in *Chicken Soup for the Traveler's Soul* ©2002.

April 21, adapted from "Real Vision," originally published in *Chicken Soup for the Mother's Soul* ©1997.

April 22, adapted from "The Swing," originally published in *Chicken Soup for the Girlfriend's Soul* ©2004.

April 23, adapted from "Good to Be Home," originally published in *Chicken Soup for the Expectant Mother's Soul* ©2000.

April 24, adapted from "A Treasure Without Price," originally published in *Chicken Soup for the Mother's Soul* ©2001.

April 25, adapted from "The Boy Who Saved Thousands of Lives," originally published in *Chicken Soup for the Writer's Soul* ©2000.

April 26, adapted from "Tale of a Sports Mom," originally published in *Chicken Soup for the Mother's Soul* ©1997.

April 27, originally published in *Chicken Soup for the Parent's Soul* ©2000.

April 28, adapted from "Japanese Good-Bye," originally published in *Chicken Soup for the Traveler's Soul* ©2002.

April 29, adapted from "To Captain Candy and the Women Who Took to the Skies," originally published in *Chicken Soup for the Mother's Soul* ©1997.

April 30, adapted from "The Face of America," reprinted with permission from *HeroicStories.com* ©2001, originally published in *Chicken Soup for the Soul of America* ©2002.

May 1, adapted from "May Baskets," originally published in *Life Lessons for Women* ©2004.

May 2, adapted from "The Heart of Paris," originally published in *Chicken Soup for the Traveler's Soul* ©2002.

May 3, adapted from "The Obsession," originally published in *Chicken Soup for the Writer's Soul* ©2000.

May 4, originally published in *Chicken Soup for the Parent's Soul* ©2000.

May 5, adapted from "Dreams Lost and Found," originally published in *Chicken Soup for the Writer's Soul* ©2000.

May 6, adapted from "Taking Control," originally published in *Chicken Soup for the Soul of America* ©2002.

May 7, adapted from "I've Fallen and I Can't Get Up!" originally published in *Chicken Soup for the Girlfriend's Soul* ©2004.

May 8, adapted from "A Dolphin Wish Fulfilled," originally published in *Chicken Soup for the Parent's Soul* ©2000.

May 9, originally published in *Chicken Soup for the Girlfriend's Soul* ©2004.

May 10, adapted from "Delayed Gratification," originally published in *Chicken Soup for the Expectant Mother's Soul* ©2000.

May 11, adapted from "Lesson in Courage," originally published in *Chicken Soup for the Expectant Mother's Soul* ©2000.

May 12, adapted from "My Traveling Companion," originally published in *Chicken Soup for the Traveler's Soul* ©2002.

May 13, adapted from "The Video of Life," originally published in *Chicken Soup for the Parent's Soul* ©2000.

May 14, originally published in *Chicken Soup for the Parent's Soul* ©2000.

May 15, adapted from "Dreams Do Come True," originally published in *Chicken Soup for the Writer's Soul* ©2000.

May 16, adapted from "Close Your Mouth, Open Your Arms," originally published in *Chicken Soup for the Mother's Soul 2* ©2001.

May 17, adapted from "The Pickle Jar," originally published in *Chicken Soup for the Parent's Soul* ©2000.

May 18, adapted from "May Basket," originally published in *Chicken Soup for the Girlfriend's Soul* ©2004.

May 19, adapted from "1,600 Articles Ago. . . ," originally published in *Chicken Soup for the Writer's Soul* ©2000.

May 20, adapted from "Daddy," originally published in *Chicken Soup for the Parent's Soul* ©2000.

May 21, originally published in *Chicken Soup for the Parent's Soul* ©2000.

May 22, adapted from "Somebody Else's Children," originally published in *Chicken Soup for the Mother's Soul 2* ©2001.

May 23, adapted from "Danny's Gift," originally published in *Chicken Soup for the Teacher's Soul* ©2002.

May 24, adapted from "True Generosity," originally published in *Chicken Soup for the Parent's Soul* ©2000.

May 25, adapted from "The Courage of the Long-Distance Writer," originally published in *Chicken Soup for the Writer's Soul* ©2000.

May 26, adapted from "I Was Born for This Job," originally published in *Chicken Soup for the Mother's Soul* ©1997.

May 27, adapted from "Bedtime Stories Across the Miles," originally published in *Chicken Soup for the Parent's Soul* ©2000.

May 28, adapted from "Joe," originally published in *Chicken Soup for the Traveler's Soul* ©2002.

May 29, originally published in *Chicken Soup for the Parent's Soul* ©2000.

May 30, adapted from "Beep if You Love America," originally published in *Chicken Soup for the Soul of America* ©2002.

May 31, adapted from "You're a Loser, Cunningham," originally published in *Chicken Soup for the Writer's Soul* ©2000.

June 1, adapted from "The Spinner Plate," originally published in *Chicken Soup for the Parent's Soul* ©2000.

June 2, adapted from "Tired?" originally published in *Chicken Soup for the Mother's Soul 2* ©2001.

June 3, adapted from "How to Write Your Way Through College," originally published in *Chicken Soup for the Writer's Soul* ©2000.

June 4, adapted from "The Tooth Fairy," originally published in *Chicken Soup for the Parent's Soul* ©2000.

June 5, adapted from "Self-Esteem at Five," originally published in *Chicken Soup for the Parent's Soul* ©2000.

June 6, originally published in *Chicken Soup for the Parent's Soul* ©2000.

June 7, adapted from "Love Notes," originally published in *Chicken Soup for the Expectant Mother's Soul* ©2000.

June 8, adapted from "In Praise of Best Girlfriends," originally published in *Chicken Soup for the Girlfriend's Soul* ©2004.

June 9, adapted from "Mommy, Please Write a Book for Me," originally published in *Chicken Soup for the Writer's Soul* ©2000.

June 10, adapted from "Keeping the Magic," originally published in *Chicken Soup for the Parent's Soul* ©2000.

June 11, adapted from "How I Want to Be Remembered," originally published in *Chicken Soup for the Writer's Soul* ©2000.

June 12, adapted from "Answering His Country's Call," originally published in *Chicken Soup for the Soul of America* ©2002.

June 13, adapted from "I'm Ready," originally published in *Chicken Soup for the Expectant Mother's Soul* ©2000.

June 14, originally published in *Chicken Soup for the Writer's Soul* ©2000.

June 15, adapted from "There Is So Much to Learn," originally published in *Chicken Soup for the Parent's Soul* ©2000.

June 16, adapted from "Half the Fun Is Getting There," originally published in *Chicken Soup for the Girlfriend's Soul* ©2004.

June 17, adapted from "Leap into Life," originally published in *Life Lessons for Women* ©2004.

June 18, adapted from "So Long Lives This," originally published in *Chicken Soup for the Writer's Soul* ©2000.

June 19, adapted from "When Mother Came to Tea," originally published in *Chicken Soup for the Mother's Soul* ©1997.

June 20, adapted from "On Becoming a Stepmother," originally published in *Chicken Soup for the Parent's Soul* ©2000.

June 21, originally published in *Chicken Soup for the Writer's Soul* ©2000.

June 22, adapted from "Write—To Conquer Your Fear," originally published in *Chicken Soup for the Writer's Soul* ©2000.

June 23, adapted from "The Light at the End of the Tunnel," originally published in *Chicken Soup for the Parent's Soul* ©2000.

June 24, adapted from "Cyberstepmother," originally published in *Chicken Soup for the Parent's Soul* ©2000.

June 25, adapted from "The Wonders of Tupperware," originally published in *Chicken Soup for the Mother's Soul 2* ©2001.

June 26, adapted from "Famous Last Words," originally published in *Chicken Soup for the Girlfriend's Soul* ©2004.

June 27, adapted from "Against All Odds," originally published in *Chicken Soup for the Parent's Soul* ©2000.

June 28, originally published in *Chicken Soup for the Writer's Soul* ©2000.

June 29, adapted from "The Miraculous Link," originally published in *Chicken Soup for the Writer's Soul* ©2000.

June 30, adapted from "Ronny's Book," originally published in *Chicken Soup for the Writer's Soul* ©2000.

July 1, adapted from "Wasting Water," originally published in *Chicken Soup for the Mother's Soul 2* ©2001.

July 2, adapted from "George and Gracie's Babies," originally published in *Chicken Soup for the Mother's Soul 2* ©2001.

July 3, adapted from "The Family Dinner," originally published in *Chicken Soup for the Mother's Soul* ©1997.

July 4, adapted from "Spouse of a Soldier," originally published in *Chicken Soup for the Military Wife's Soul* ©2005.

July 5, adapted from "My Sister's Shadow," originally published in *Chicken Soup for the Sister's Soul* ©2002.

July 6, originally published in *Chicken Soup for the Working Woman's Soul* ©2003.

July 7, adapted from "Promises to Keep," originally published in *Chicken Soup for the Teacher's Soul* ©2002.

July 8, adapted from "Dance with Me," originally published in *Chicken Soup for the Mother's Soul* ©1997.

July 9, adapted from "A Musical Eye-Opener," originally published in *Chicken Soup for the Caregiver's Soul* ©2004.

July 10, adapted from "Step on a Crack, Bring Your Mother Back," originally published in *Chicken Soup for the Mother's Soul 2* ©2001.

July 11, adapted from "Wisdom of the Birds," originally published in *Life Lessons for Women* ©2004.

July 12, adapted from "Maya's Smile," originally published in *Chicken Soup for the Parent's Soul* ©2000.

July 13, adapted from "When All Hope Is Lost," originally published in *Chicken Soup for the Caregiver's Soul* ©2004.

July 14, originally published in *Chicken Soup for the Working Woman's Soul* ©2003.

July 15, adapted from "Permission to Fail," originally published in *Chicken Soup for the Teacher's Soul* ©2002.

July 16, adapted from "All Those Years," originally published in *Chicken Soup for the Mother's Soul* ©1997.

July 17, adapted from "Keeping the High Watch," originally published in *Chicken Soup for the Expectant Mother's Soul* ©2000.

July 18, adapted from "The End of Childhood," originally published in *Chicken Soup for the Parent's Soul* ©2000.

July 19, adapted from "An Indescribable Gift," originally published in *Chicken Soup for the Mother's Soul* ©1997.

July 20, adapted from "It's All Relative," originally published in *Chicken Soup for the Sister's Soul* ©2002.

July 21, adapted from "Nathan's Upgrade," originally published in *Chicken Soup for the Traveler's Soul* ©2002.

July 22, adapted from "Daydreams Die," originally published in *Life Lessons for Women* ©2004.

July 23, originally published in *Chicken Soup for the Working Woman's Soul* ©2003.

July 24, adapted from "Forever, for Always, and No Matter What!" originally published in *Chicken Soup for the Mother's Soul* ©1997.

July 25, adapted from "Saving Him," originally published in *Chicken Soup for the Caregiver's Soul* ©2004.

July 26, adapted from "A Turkish Delight," originally published in *Chicken Soup for the Traveler's Soul* ©2002.

July 27, adapted from "Miracle Wallet," originally published in *Chicken Soup for the Military Wife's Soul* ©2005.

July 28, adapted from "Squeeze My Hand and I'll Tell You That I Love You," originally published in *Chicken Soup for the Mother's Soul* ©1997.

July 29, adapted from "This Space," originally published in *Chicken Soup for the Caregiver's Soul* ©2004.

July 30, adapted from "Watching Me Go," originally published in *Chicken Soup for the Parent's Soul* ©2000.

July 31, originally published in *Chicken Soup for the Working Woman's Soul* ©2003.

August 1, adapted from "When a Mother Blows Out 75 Candles," originally published in *Chicken Soup for the Mother's Soul* ©1997.

August 2, adapted from "At Every Turn," originally published in *Chicken Soup for the Sister's Soul* ©2002.

August 3, adapted from "Goals and Dreams—A Winning Team," originally published in *Chicken Soup for the Teacher's Soul* ©2002.

August 4, adapted from "The Christmas I Was Rich," originally published in *Chicken Soup for the Mother's Soul 2* ©2001.

August 5, adapted from "Too Late," originally published in *Chicken Soup for the Caregiver's Soul* ©2004.

August 6, adapted from "Letters of Hope," originally published in *Chicken Soup for the Military Wife's Soul* ©2005.

August 7, adapted from "Defining Love," originally published in *Chicken Soup for the Parent's Soul* ©2000.

August 8, originally published in *Chicken Soup for the Mother and Daughter Soul* ©2002.

August 9, adapted from "Miss You, Love You," originally published in *Chicken Soup for the Traveler's Soul* ©2002.

August 10, adapted from "Celebrating My Mother," originally published in *Chicken Soup for the Mother's Soul* ©1997.

August 11, adapted from "Grandma's Garden," originally published in *Chicken Soup for the Mother's Soul* ©1997.

August 12, adapted from "Who Wants to Be a Millionaire Anyway?" originally published in *Life Lessons for Women* ©2004.

August 13, adapted from "Love's Own Language," originally published in *Chicken Soup for the Caregiver's Soul* ©2004.

August 14, adapted from "I Will Always Love You," originally published in *Chicken Soup for the Teacher's Soul* ©2002.

August 15, originally published in *Chicken Soup for the Mother and Daughter Soul* ©2002.

August 16, adapted from "The Quiet Hero," originally published in *Chicken Soup for the Mother's Soul* ©1997.

August 17, adapted from "I'm Not Your Slave," originally published in *Chicken Soup for the Parent's Soul* ©2000.

August 18, adapted from "Follow Your Heart," originally published in *Life Lessons for Women* ©2004.

August 19, adapted from "She Looks Like Us," originally published in *Chicken Soup for the Mother's Soul* ©1997.

August 20, adapted from "The Bungee That Binds," originally published in *Chicken Soup for the Parent's Soul* ©2000.

August 21, adapted from "Dear Precious Husband," originally published in *Chicken Soup for the Caregiver's Soul* ©2004.

August 22, adapted from "My Daughter, My Teacher," originally published in *Chicken Soup for the Mother's Soul* ©1997.

August 23, adapted from "Leaving Home," originally published in *Chicken Soup for the Mother's Soul 2* ©2001.

August 24, originally published in *Chicken Soup for the Mother and Daughter Soul* ©2002.

August 25, adapted from "Ticketless Travel," originally published in *Chicken Soup for the Traveler's Soul* ©2002.

August 26, adapted from "Hello, Beautiful," originally published in *Chicken Soup for the Military Wife's Soul* ©2005.

August 27, adapted from "View from an Empty Nest," originally published in *Life Lessons for Women* ©2004.

August 28, adapted from "Food for Thought," originally published in *Chicken Soup for the Caregiver's Soul* ©2004.

August 29, adapted from "A Gift of Love," originally published in *Chicken Soup for the Expectant Mother's Soul* ©2000.

August 30, originally published in *Chicken Soup for the Bride's Soul* ©2004.

August 31, adapted from "Girls' Weekend," originally published in *Chicken Soup for the Sister's Soul* ©2002.

September 1, adapted from "I Don't Want a New Baby," originally published in *Chicken Soup for the Mother's Soul* ©1997.

September 2, adapted from "Mercy," originally published in *Chicken Soup for the Military Wife's Soul* ©2005.

September 3, adapted from "To Have and to Hold," originally published in *Chicken Soup for the Mother's Soul 2* ©2001.

September 4, adapted from "Born a Teacher," originally published in *Chicken Soup for the Teacher's Soul* ©2002.

September 5, adapted from "Beach Day," originally published in *Chicken Soup for the Sister's Soul* ©2002.

September 6, adapted from "Level the Playing Field," originally published in *Chicken Soup for the Caregiver's Soul* ©2004.

September 7, adapted from "The Question," originally published in *Chicken Soup for the Mother's Soul 2* ©2001.

September 8, adapted from "Teen Wisdom," originally published in *Chicken Soup for the Parent's Soul* ©2000.

September 9, adapted from "Hearts Across the World," originally published in *Chicken Soup for the Mother's Soul* ©1997.

September 10, adapted from "The Travelers," originally published in *Chicken Soup for the Caregiver's Soul* ©2004.

September 11, adapted from "A Perfect Son," originally published in *Chicken Soup for the Mother's Soul* ©1997.

September 12, adapted from "Angel in Uniform," originally published in *Chicken Soup for the Mother's Soul* ©1997.

September 13, adapted from "The Sleeping Room," originally published in *Chicken Soup for the Traveler's Soul* ©2002.

September 14, adapted from "Welcome, Levi!" originally published in *Chicken Soup for the Parent's Soul* ©2000.

September 15, adapted from "The Mouth That Roared," originally published in *Chicken Soup for the Expectant Mother's Soul* ©2000.

September 16, adapted from "No Response," originally published in *Chicken Soup for the Caregiver's Soul* ©2004.

September 17, adapted from "Daddy's Angels," originally published in *Chicken Soup for the Military Wife's Soul* ©2005.

September 18, adapted from "The Tooth Fairy," originally published in *Chicken Soup for the Mother's Soul* ©1997.

September 19, adapted from "Life After Death," originally published in *Life Lessons for Women* ©2004.

September 20, adapted from "Different," originally published in *Chicken Soup for the Sister's Soul* ©2002.

September 21, adapted from "Comic-Book Solomon," originally published in *Chicken Soup for the Parent's Soul* ©2000.

September 22, adapted from "That's Just Roscoe," originally published in *Chicken Soup for the Teacher's Soul* ©2002.

September 23, adapted from "Finding Her There," originally published in *Chicken Soup for the Mother's Soul* ©1997.

September 24, adapted from "We Almost Did That," originally published in *Chicken Soup for the Traveler's Soul* ©2002.

September 25, adapted from "Long-Distance Vitamins," originally published in *Chicken Soup for the Caregiver's Soul* ©2004.

September 26, adapted from "If I Were Lucky," originally published in *Life Lessons for Women* ©2004.

September 27, adapted from "Enjoy Your Baby," originally published in *Chicken Soup for the Expectant Mother's Soul* ©2000.

September 28, adapted from "Sticks and Stones," originally published in *Life Lessons for Women* ©2004.

September 29, adapted from "Land Without Mirrors," originally published in *Chicken Soup for the Traveler's Soul* ©2002.

September 30, adapted from "Inseparable," originally published in *Chicken Soup for the Sister's Soul* ©2002.

October 1, adapted from "Little Marie," originally published in *Chicken Soup for the Grandparent's Soul* ©2002.

October 2, adapted from "Sheba," originally published in *Chicken Soup for the Cat and Dog Lover's Soul* ©1999.

October 3, adapted from "After the Tears," originally published in *Chicken Soup for the Mother's Soul 2* ©2001.

October 4, adapted from "The Starter Jar," originally published in *Chicken Soup for the Girlfriend's Soul* ©2004.

October 5, originally published in *Chicken Soup for the Bride's Soul* ©2004.

October 6, adapted from "Raising My Sights," originally published in *Chicken Soup for the Grandparent's Soul* ©2002.

October 7, adapted from "One More Task," originally published in *Chicken Soup for the Girlfriend's Soul* ©2004.

October 8, adapted from "A Turning Point," originally published in *Life Lessons for Women* ©2004.

October 9, adapted from "Cori's Beads," originally published in *Chicken Soup for the Parent's Soul* ©2000.

October 10, adapted from "Making a 'Pottment," originally published in *Chicken Soup for the Writer's Soul* ©2000.

October 11, adapted from "Need a Hand?" originally published in *Chicken Soup for the Teacher's Soul* ©2002.

October 12, adapted from "The Necklace," originally published in *Chicken Soup for the Girlfriend's Soul* ©2004.

October 13, originally published in *Chicken Soup for the Romantic Soul* ©2002.

October 14, adapted from "The Priceless Gift," originally published in *Chicken Soup for the Grandparent's Soul* ©2002.

October 15, adapted from "They'll Be Fine," originally published in *Chicken Soup for the Expectant Mother's Soul* ©2000.

October 16, adapted from "Playing Cupid," originally published in *Chicken Soup for the Sister's Soul* ©2002.

October 17, adapted from "Proud to Be a Nurse," originally published in *Chicken Soup for the Nurse's Soul* ©2001.

October 18, adapted from "Great Answer," originally published in *Chicken Soup for the Teacher's Soul* ©2002.

October 19, adapted from "Monsters Under the Bed," originally published in *Chicken Soup for the Parent's Soul* ©2000.

October 20, adapted from "Sister's Song," originally published in *Chicken Soup for the Sister's Soul* ©2002.

October 21, originally published in *Chicken Soup for the Romantic Soul* ©2002.

October 22, adapted from "Dreams Have a Price," originally published in *Chicken Soup for the Writer's Soul* ©2000.

October 23, adapted from "Unexpected Blessings," originally published in *Chicken Soup for the Expectant Mother's Soul* ©2000.

October 24, adapted from "All in a Day's Work," previously appeared in *Chicken Soup for the Soul at Work*, originally published in *Chicken Soup for the Nurse's Soul* ©2001.

October 25, adapted from "A Sister Is . . . ," originally published in *Chicken Soup for the Sister's Soul* ©2002.

October 26, adapted from "Church Dog," originally published in *Chicken Soup for the Cat and Dog Lover's Soul* ©1999.

October 27, adapted from "Why Choose Teaching?" originally published in *Chicken Soup for the Teacher's Soul* ©2002.

October 28, originally published in *Chicken Soup for the Romantic Soul* ©2002.

October 29, adapted from "Love of a Child," originally published in *Chicken Soup for the Parent's Soul* ©2000.

October 30, adapted from "Full Circle," originally published in *Life Lessons for Women* ©2004.

October 31, adapted from "Be Ready When Your Editor Calls," originally published in *Chicken Soup for the Writer's Soul* ©2000.

November 1, adapted from "Can't Let Go," originally published in *Chicken Soup for the Military Wife's Soul* ©2005.

November 2, adapted from "The Journey," originally published in *Chicken Soup for the Single's Soul* ©1999.

November 3, adapted from "The Love Squad," originally published in *Chicken Soup for the Girlfriend's Soul* ©2004.

November 4, adapted from "A Year Behind Sister and Forty," originally published in *Chicken Soup for the Sister's Soul* ©2002.

November 5, adapted from "Mum and the Volkswagen," originally published in *Chicken Soup for the Mother's Soul 2* ©2001.

November 6, originally published in *Chicken Soup for the Caregiver's Soul* ©2004.

November 7, adapted from "Angels Shop at Wal-Mart," originally published in *Chicken Soup for the Military Wife's Soul* ©2005.

November 8, adapted from "Something to Make Me Happy," originally published in *Chicken Soup for the Parent's Soul* ©2000.

November 9, adapted from "Message in a Mug," originally published in *Chicken Soup for the Single's Soul* ©1999.

November 10, adapted from "Papa's Gift," originally published in *Chicken Soup for the Writer's Soul* ©2000.

November 11, adapted from "Truly Blessed," originally published in *Chicken Soup for the Sister's Soul* ©2002.

November 12, adapted from "Mixed Blessings," originally published in *Chicken Soup for the Writer's Soul* ©2000.

November 13, adapted from "A Real Home," originally published in *Chicken Soup for the Mother's Soul 2* ©2001.

November 14, adapted from "A Precious Gift," originally published in *Chicken Soup for the Expectant Mother's Soul* ©2000.

November 15, originally published in *Chicken Soup for the Mother's Soul 2* ©2001.

November 16, adapted from "Miriam's Umbrella," originally published in *Chicken Soup for the Parent's Soul* ©2000.

November 17, adapted from "A Bunch of Violets," originally published in *Chicken Soup for the Single's Soul* ©1999.

November 18, adapted from "A Forever Friend," originally published in *Chicken Soup for the Girlfriend's Soul* ©2004.

November 19, adapted from "A Military Family," originally published in *Chicken Soup for the Military Wife's Soul* ©2005.

November 20, adapted from "My Son, My Grandson," originally published in *Chicken Soup for the Parent's Soul* ©2000.

November 21, adapted from "The Pencil Box," originally published in *Chicken Soup for the Mother's Soul 2* ©2001.

November 22, originally published in *Chicken Soup for the Single's Soul* ©1999.

November 23, adapted from "Of Yellow-Haired Dolls and Ugly Clay Bowls," originally published in *Chicken Soup for the Parent's Soul* ©2000.

November 24, adapted from "No Time for Dreams," originally published in *Chicken Soup for the Single's Soul* ©1999.

November 25, adapted from "A Simple Act of Kindness," originally published in *Chicken Soup for the Military Wife's Soul* ©2005.

November 26, adapted from "The Other Mother," originally published in *Chicken Soup for the Parent's Soul* ©2000.

November 27, adapted from "Everything He Had," originally published in *Chicken Soup for the Single's Soul* ©1999.

November 28, originally published in *Chicken Soup for the Single's Soul* ©1999.

November 29, adapted from "My Family Was Separated," originally published in *Chicken Soup for the Sister's Soul* ©2002.

November 30, adapted from "The Book of Friendship," originally published in *Chicken Soup for the Girlfriend's Soul* ©2004.

December 1, adapted from "What Day Is Today?" originally published in *Chicken Soup for the Nurse's Soul* ©2001.

December 2, adapted from "Three Men and a …," originally published in *Chicken Soup for the Traveler's Soul* ©2002.

December 3, originally published in *Chicken Soup for the Single's Soul* ©1999.

December 4, adapted from "Earning Her Wings," originally published in *Chicken Soup for the Caregiver's Soul* ©2004.

December 5, adapted from "Where's My Little Sister?" originally published in *Chicken Soup for the Sister's Soul* ©2002.

December 6, adapted from "The Mailbox," originally published in *Chicken Soup for the Mother's Soul 2* ©2001.

December 7, adapted from "Melts in Your Heart, Not in Your Hand," originally published in *Chicken Soup for the Girlfriend's Soul* ©2004.

December 8, adapted from "A Forever Kind of Love," originally published in *Chicken Soup for the Nurse's Soul* ©2001.

December 9, adapted from "To See a Volcano," originally published in *Chicken Soup for the Traveler's Soul* ©2002.

December 10, adapted from "Paid in Full," originally published in *Chicken Soup for the Single's Soul* ©1999.

December 11, originally published in *Chicken Soup for the Grandparent's Soul* ©2002.

December 12, adapted from "The Drawer Wouldn't Close," originally published in *Chicken Soup for the Single's Soul* ©1999.

December 13, adapted from "Precious in My Eyes," originally published in *Chicken Soup for the Sister's Soul* ©2002.

December 14, adapted from "Big Problems, Little Miracles," originally published in *Chicken Soup for the Girlfriend's Soul* ©2004.

December 15, adapted from "Next to My Heart," originally published in *Chicken Soup for the Mother's Soul 2* ©2001.

December 16, adapted from "A Little White Lie," originally published in *Chicken Soup for the Sister's Soul* ©2002.

December 17, adapted from "L'Air du Temps," originally published in *Chicken Soup for the Traveler's Soul* ©2002.

December 18, adapted from "Long-Distance Sister," originally published in *Chicken Soup for the Sister's Soul* ©2002.

December 19, originally published in *Chicken Soup for the Grandparent's Soul* ©2002.

December 20, adapted from "A Single Act of Love," originally published in *Chicken Soup for the Nurse's Soul* ©2001.

December 21, adapted from "Not Just Another Birthday," originally published in *Chicken Soup for the Sister's Soul* ©2002.

December 22, adapted from "The Art of Traveling," originally published in *Chicken Soup for the Traveler's Soul* ©2002.

December 23, originally published in *Chicken Soup for the Grandparent's Soul* ©2002.